A FUTURE FOR HOMO ⌐...

by
Peter Garrington

The attempt of an old Hodge[1] to save an endangered species from destroying itself and its environment, by introducing an economic system that meets its needs and rebuilds and preserves its environment, producing a near Utopian State where basic human rights are available to all.

To the Oldie,

From an old Hodge with best wishes

Peter - Garrington

March 1995.

---

[1] Hodge - an old English word meaning a countryman or rustic.

First Published in Great Britain in 1994

Orchard Publications
2 Orchard Close, Chudleigh, Newton Abbot, Devon. TQ13 0LR
Telephone: (01626) 852714

British Library Cataloguing in Publication Data
CIP Catalogue Record for this book is available
from the British Library

ISBN 1 898964 07 6

Designed, Typeset and Printed for Orchard Publications by
Swift Print
2, High Street, Dawlish, Devon. EX7 9HP

CONTENTS

The Present Disastrous Situation

The earth, its atmosphere and crust are finite resources that by a slow evolutionary process, have formed over millions of years. Within the limits of present human knowledge it is unique in the cosmos, and no species of flora or fauna can exploit or destroy the earth indefinitely without destroying themselves. The environment in which the present flora and fauna have grown up is very delicately balanced between moisture, temperature and nutrients that enable a species to survive. Destroy that environment and it will take tens of thousands of years for it to recover, indeed the species that caused the destruction may never re-emerge.

In 1985, just before he was elected Secretary General of the Communist Party, Mikhail Gorbachov told the Supreme Assembly of the Soviet Union "We cannot go on living like this –". He was talking of course of the Communist State, but his words applied to the species Homo sapiens across the whole earth, especially those in the Western World. Homo sapiens is the most predaceous and destructive species evolution has yet produced, making the Dinosaurs look like struggling amateurs.

When the population of a species exhausts the environment that maintains it, they start a mass migration to find a new environment which will provide sustenance for its numbers. The Lemming species, a vole like rodent of northern and Arctic regions of Europe, Asia and North America is well known for this, often tumbling over cliffs into rivers or the sea and destroying themselves in the process. One has only to travel on a motorway or autobahn and watch drivers in the fast lane to see the species Homo sapiens doing the same thing, only they sit in metal boxes on four wheels to achieve the same results. The river or abyss the Homos fall into is of their own making through overpopulation and using a monetary system that encourages the destruction of their environment. The present methods of creating wealth

1

automatically involve the removal, without replacement, of part of the earth's crust or atmosphere.

Because Homo sapiens has an enlarged brain and a well developed memory and can think quickly, it has an erroneous concept that it controls its environment and can ignore the slow process of evolution. But its body and its functions are the same as it evolved in the Pliocene age, and except for the enlargement of the brain, little has altered since that period. It was devised to be active, running and walking all the time, and kept healthy by such activities. The eyes were intended to look great distances and be constantly focusing. The digestive system needs frequent shaking to function properly; it was not intended to sit for long periods in motor cars, at computers, typewriters, watching television as modern Western living demands.

In the process of evolution of a species it had to be capable of obtaining energy from its food otherwise it did not reproduce itself and became extinct. When it destroyed the surroundings it lived in, it had to migrate to other areas that contained the moisture and nutrients that it required to sustain itself. This is still true of all species including Homo sapiens and leads to mass migrations. Political and economic factors of an area are helping speed such movements of people. The Chinese, Indian and African migrants in the Western World are evidence of this, just as the Lemmings out of Arctica, the Wildebeest in Africa or the Elks of the northern hemisphere.

All energy for life originates from the sun. In the process of evolution the earliest forms of living tissues developed a substance now known as chlorophyll, which traps the energy of the sun by a process known as photosynthesis. Chlorophyll is the green pigment in all plants which use water, various chemical nutrients and carbon dioxide from the air to produce sugars and starches. All other forms of life are dependent on this food to produce the energy they require to live, photosynthesis has fuelled the global evolution of fauna and flora to this day. Plant eating animals (Herbivores) are the most numerous converters of plants into flesh and muscle. The predators on herbivores, including Homo sapiens, require these as an essential part of their food chain, and must either alter their feeding habits or become extinct.

The energy of plants and their power to feed has driven a natural process of evolvement and the creation of the earth's environment, which now drives modern industry, for man who has learnt to use fossil fuels, which all came from plants over a long period of geological time. The giant Redwood trees (Sequoya) of America have been built out of the sun's energy over a period of two thousand years. One stupid Homo with a chain saw can destroy it in a few hours. He will have a very long wait for the next one to cut after he has felled the last one.

In the process of evolution millions of species have evolved and many have become extinct because of the destruction of their environment by themselves or by geological changes – heat, cold, flooding, volcanic eruptions etc. The first ancestors of Homo sapiens appeared about two million years B.C., a mere yesterday compared with the estimated age of the earth – 4,750,000,000 B.C. give or take a year or two. The first evidence of ancestors of Homo sapiens dates from about 180,000 B.C. found in the Neanderthal valley near Dusseldorf in Germany. They became almost extinct in the first cold phase about 40,000 B.C. By the second cold phase 30,000 B.C. Homo sapiens was showing advances of great significance with small knife blades, engraving tools, paintings and wall sculptures.

The last Ice age left Europe about 8,000 B.C. and settled agriculture started to develop in the Middle East. Modern society has developed therefore over the last 10,000 years. If it continues with its present rate of destruction of the earth's environment it may not last another one thousand years. Man with his highly developed brain and the memory it contains has learnt to misuse energy to destroy his environment at an increasingly terrifying rate. The object of this writer is to make the control of energy usage the basic principal of human society, and so possibly enable the species to continue for a longer period.

Geological evolution takes about 1,000 years to form one inch of topsoil from the subsoil and bedrock. To sustain plants and trees ten to twelve inches of topsoil are necessary, and it must be organically balanced and protected so it is not eroded by wind and water. Productive plants need time to develop, annuals produce seed in one year and biennials in two years. Perennials will continue doing it once established, while trees and shrubs take longer periods to produce seeds. A mature English oak takes 300-400 years to mature, the American Redwood 1,500-2,000 years to do so, while the Mahoganies and other hardwoods in the rain forest take between 400-800 years. Homo sapiens with a bulldozer can destroy 10,000 years of topsoil production in an afternoon, or with a chainsaw can cut 300 to 2,000 years of growth in the same time.

In the last three hundred years the development of the Industrial Society and the economic system needed to run it has destroyed more of the world's environment than that of the previous 30,000 years. Not only is the earth's surface being destroyed but the atmosphere above it, and the pollution of the surface waters are poisoning the whole Eco-system. Two thirds of the world's population are underfed or starving, so-called food surplus cannot be distributed because the economic system cannot cope with the demands that distribution would involve. A system that developed to facilitate the exchange of goods no longer functions because a few hold the economic units and the many who need them to survive cannot gain access to them. This is leading to migrations on a mass scale from the areas that do not have the monetary units to those that have. This is basic survival instincts in action.

The species Homo sapiens has always been extremely successful at increasing its numbers. Its enlarged brain and so called intelligence has enabled the species to do this; the stronger and more intelligent in a social group have become the leaders or politicians, and have organised the group to protect its own territory, take over the territory of other groups, and confiscate their possessions and wealth. This is a similar behaviour pattern to that of most other species which have evolved, but Homo sapiens was more vicious and successful. War and conquest have been an essential part of society development with the wars of the Greeks, the

Romans, and many other groups; the Spanish, Portuguese, French, British, Germans and Russians continued the system until today.

The Chinese, a society that has existed longer than all others was highly organised and grew; it now has a quarter of the world's population. In the course of their development they invented gunpowder, which has been one way of controlling population, but wasteful of environmental assets by doing so to mature members of society. It is a great pity they did not invent a successful form of contraception that would diminish the use of environmental assets. For long periods in Chinese history the destruction of infant girls has been a method of containing population growth up to recent times. The greater the growth of the Chinese population the poorer the country has become in spite of so much human energy being available to it. Their less numerous neighbours in Japan have been more successful in the world of finance, but in spreading their wealth across the world population they will soon suffer the same financial reverses which other wealthy nations have.

Political power is about organising society to have their basic needs of energy, housing, and standards of living matched by the wealth of that society. Once this fails then unrest will either have to be controlled by oppressive force or by meeting the demands of the people. The speed of modern communication by television and radio has weakened the power of politicians and no one now is an island, all are part of the main society of the world. Recent developments in what was the Soviet Union and the Middle East have enhanced the standing of the United Nations as an organisation for social and economic progress, it has to play a major part in the controlling of the activities of Homo sapiens if the world environment is to be repaired, improved and to survive another thousand years or so.

Religions have also played a part in the evolution of society. The overactive human brain has always sought solutions to problems by belief in some supreme power, be it Confucianism, Hindu, Muslim, Christian or any other known form of worship. The Inca civilisation in the Andes of south America rightly recognised the central power of the sun in human affairs and worshipped it as a god, until they in turn were conquered by the Spaniards. The proliferation of the Human race has been the aim of some religions and has greatly speeded up the overpopulation of the world by Homo sapiens. This has always proved to be one of the most difficult aspects of trying to control population numbers. Large numbers of the world's people have died in wars fought over religious beliefs, this is an expensive and idiotic way to control population numbers, seen as a threat to a religion or society.

The greatest absurdity that Homo sapiens has developed in the past three to four hundred years has been the financial system. The real worth of communities is the energy and skills of their people and the financial system should enable them to trade those assets for goods and necessities that they require in every day life. The energy and skill of the people should be the unit of the financial system and enable goods to flow around without restriction. Money was developed to facilitate trade. Unfortunately it has now reached the point where the unit of exchange dominates trade instead of facilitating it and financially poor communities are full of people with skills and energy to make goods for selling, but the currency is not available for others to buy them. Some of these people feel worthless because they are unable to exchange their services for units of exchange, an alternative unit of exchange has to be developed quickly to stimulate world trade. The present systems are now so inefficient and failing to serve the needs of human society that two thirds of the world population is underfed, and living in extreme discomfort and poverty, while the other third controls the so called wealth and the economic system by which the world trades. This has always led to mass migrations from the poor to the rich areas.

The rich mixture of ethnic communities found in the Western world shows that these migrations have been going on for a long time, nowhere is this more clearly illustrated than in America, and to a lesser extent, the United Kingdom. For third world countries to obtain finance they must borrow from the International and western banking systems, this involves them in high interest payments; these they find they cannot meet and so default on their debts. The Banks have to write off these debts and so increase their interest charges to other borrowers. With the break-up of the Soviet Union and the strain this is going to place on the world banking system it will quickly lead to the breakdown of the present international financial exchange mechanism as banks run out of assets to meet the burgeoning cash demand. Once these assets are used up, and the banks' liabilities are too great to be recouped, then world bankruptcy is the end of that story and chaos will erupt world wide.

How and why has the financial system become so dominant and yet so inefficient? This stems from the tremendous growth of the world's population and the necessity for world trade to maintain that population; the economic system was not designed to cope with such numbers and volume of trade. The evolution of currencies came from coins based on so-called precious metals in the middle ages, as various Empires came and went so their currency dominated the trading economy of the time – the golden doubloons of the Spanish Empire, the silver Maria Theresia Dollar of the Hapsburg Empire, the golden sovereigns of the British Empire; even the Shekels of the Middle East, so loved by Shylock, the heartless userer in Shakespeare's *"Merchant of Venice"*. As trade grew, coins were difficult to trade with and soon the coffee houses of London became the centres of finance, issuing Notes of credit that enabled entrepreneurs to trade and obtain goods before payment. Out of this hit-and-miss system developed the vast banking systems of today. The currency no longer relates to human everyday needs and credit is given to the most dubious of characters such as Dictators, the Mafia, crafty entrepreneurs, gunrunners and drug smugglers without any consideration as to what it is to be used for and whether it will be repaid. The collapse of various financial enterprises in recent times has only served to expose the weakness of the system. The world financial markets are really frenzied gambling shops that bear little relationship to human needs and world trade. It is essential now to start a scientifically based unit of world currency based on human needs and designed to preserve the world environment.

But the sun still shines and the vast and ever growing world population, even if underfed still generate a lot of energy. The

7

limited assets of the world that sustain global, human and environmental existence have to be maintained, improved and restored all the time. The world financial system must be central to this; energy must be conserved not wasted and human life respected, not sacrificed to monetary needs. This means improving the lifestyle of two thirds of the world and restraining the excesses of lifestyle at present practised in the Western world, and by the more affluent of the world in general.

If Homo sapiens is to survive more then a further thousand years then the financial system must enable him to do it by maintaining and continually improving the environment he lives in involving a detailed knowledge of the essentials of the environment, and how each individual human functions, and sustains itself in that environment. This knowledge has to be passed on to succeeding generations and sufficient finance has to be continually available to do this. Future generations must do this by living according to the old farming adage "Live each day as if it is your last, but farm as if you are going to live for ever." Humans must all treat the world as their farm and hand it onto the next generation in a better state than when they took it over – this, sadly, is not the position at the end of the Twentieth Century.

2

The Essentials Of Existence For Homo Sapiens

Fortunately for Homo sapiens, Human and scientific knowledge has advanced sufficiently for the basic essentials of life to be thoroughly understood and artificial environments can be produced, when demand requires it, at great cost, e.g. air and space travel, air conditioning buildings, life support machines etc. But a great deal of this knowledge is not commonly available or known to the man in the street, otherwise in these populated city streets of today no one would venture out for fear of the health risk. The basic conditions of survival taught to Servicemen in the past still apply, "A body can exist for three minutes without air, three days without water and three weeks without food". After these periods normal functions of the body are disrupted and can quickly cease.

Water has been the key compound in the evolution of the world as it is at present known. As the surface of the earth cooled, water was formed, the cold early atmosphere of the earth met the warmth of the cooling surface, cloud was condensed, moisture dropped quickly as rain. In the process of evolution this water was pulled by gravity to the lowest points on the surface, seas and oceans started to form. In time where these seas were warmed by escaping heat from the earth's surface and the sun's rays very simple and primitive forms of life were formed, living cells contained mineral salts, a nucleus and a protective skin began to evolve. The rest was a matter of a very long time, but the essential element as a result was water, aided and abetted by the warmth, sunshine, and basic minerals from the earth's surface.

It is the use of water that will determine the continued existence of the species Homo sapiens: Western society and Industry across the world has become profligate in its use, of all the earth's resources it is without doubt the resource that will terminate the existence of man on the planet. Water is continually pulled downwards into the earth's surface by gravity, it is rapidly affected by temperature, too cold and it becomes ice, too hot and it becomes evaporated into steam. If the earth warms up, as man is helping it to do, then the vast ice layers at the poles and high glaciers on mountain tops will melt and the oceans rise, flooding large areas of flat sea level land across the globe. In time the warming will lead to the evaporation of the seas and the warmed earth surface will suck in even more water, thus seas and rivers will dry up. This is already happening in many parts of the earth. Should the atmosphere start rapidly to cool down (another ice age) then seas and rivers will freeze and become ice, then Homo sapiens and many other species will have to migrate to warmer climates as happened in the last ice age 30,000 years ago.

All other plants and animals on earth also depend on the surface water. Where man removes or uses that surface water then the local species depending on it die and cease to exist in that area. The use of energy from fossil fuels to run machines has speeded up this process in the last century, and is gathering momentum across the world today. The destruction of wetlands, temperate and rain forests mean many other species are endangered and will disappear for ever. Surface and ground water is the key to all life and man must use his knowledge and technology to preserve its availability. Plants and animals in a specific area have evolved because of the area "water table". This is the depth below the surface that water is found throughout the year, the surface of a pond or river is the exposed water table for that area. The roots of plants, and thirsty animals must go down to that level to obtain the moisture they need to exist.

The presence of water in a plant or animal body is essential for the transfer of nutrients and waste products around their structure, water acts as a lubricant for the nutrients to move from one plant or animal cell to another by the process known as osmosis. This is the method by which chemicals move through the semi-permeable membrane of the cell until the chemicals are equal in level of strength on each side of that membrane. As the cell dries up so the process slows down as does the flow of nutrients or waste products. Dehydration is the commonest cause of illness and death to living tissue, a plant or animal, if it dries out, can be killed by its own waste products. Television pictures over the past few years have been showing this process going on in all the drought and war stricken regions of the modern world.

Because water is so basic to life then its purity is a key factor in maintaining that life in plants and animals. In the natural sequence of evolution certain diseases have used water to transfer from one host to another, be it in the form of viruses, bacteria, larva, eggs or larger forms of living species such as amoeba or worms. But Industry and modern civilisation have rapidly become the greatest threat to the purity of water with the use of chemicals in factories and on the land, and the discharge of untreated sewage or sewage by-products into water courses, seas, or indirectly polluting the atmosphere in the form of acid rain. With the spread of human activity there are few places left in the world where the purity of water can be guaranteed. Purifying effluent and water supplies is a high cost, high energy-use operation placing a considerable strain on the financial resources of the world monetary system.

Any activity of Homo sapiens that disturbs the earth's surface will affect the water table of that area, the foundations of a house, a trench for a water supply, a cutting for a railway or road, or the stripping of coal or gravel from the surface can all do this. Perhaps the greatest danger in this respect that lowers the water table is the ability of modern man to bore deep into the earth's surface, as happens in making boreholes for deep water supplies, oil or gas wells to extract the latter products for fossil fuels, also the sinking of deep mines for fuel and mineral extraction. The deep penetration of the surface cuts through the water table and allows it to drain down into the earth deeper than previously. A good example of this is the drying up of agricultural land and rivers and streams in eastern England, where human water supplies have come to depend on boreholes. The rainfall is now inadequate to maintain the water table at the shallow depth that plants and trees require for their existence, hence this area of England and other parts of Europe where water demands are high, are drying out, losing vegetation and will eventually become desert areas unless the process is stopped.

The makeup and the movement of the atmosphere on the earth's surface is also essential for the continuation of the environment and the existence of mankind. All life is dependent on the oxygen within the atmosphere, and plants produce that oxygen, but water vapour or humidity of the air also plays an essential part in maintaining life. Since the beginning of evolution the water and atmosphere have worked together to speed up the process of existence of all life forms, including human beings. Water is the main environment of fish and many marine mammals but that water has to be pure and unpolluted by man. The recent oil disasters at sea have shown this to the rest of the world only too well through the mass media.

Combustion in any form, be it in fires, furnaces, internal combustion engines, gas turbines etc., all require oxygen from the air to take place, thus all combustion reduces the amount of oxygen in the atmosphere and increases the level of carbon dioxide which will not sustain any form of life. Man's continual and increasing use of combustion has done the greatest damage to the earth's environment. The burning of rain and temperate forests, the excessive use of fossil fuels, especially petrol and diesel speeded up the process in the last hundred years, more than at any time since Homo sapiens existed on earth. What is more disastrous is that it has led to a vast de-vegetation of the earth's surface which has greatly speeded up the destruction of the atmosphere, for plants are the only means of producing life-giving oxygen for the continual survival of the present environment.

The pollution of the atmosphere, in the same way as the pollution of the water supply, is now greatly endangering the essential role of air in the maintenance of the living environment. Excessive carbon dioxide and sulphur dioxide (both products of combustion) greatly affect the ability of Homo sapiens to perform and work. Under still atmospheric conditions in times of heatwaves the increase in chest and breathing problems is pronounced in many cities across the world. This is entirely due to the burning of fossil fuels in a still environment leading to people having to take precautions to keep these harmful gases from their lungs. Sulphur dioxide in contact with damp in the atmosphere, eg. rain and mist, is acid in nature and is the main cause of acid rain; in many parts of Eastern and Western Europe and America the acidity of rain falling on trees, shrubs, and crops is causing the slowing down of growth and the destruction of forest trees. This process increases in close proximity to power stations, industrial plants, airfields etc., where the concentration of acid rain is greatest, a jet engined plane taking off under full throttle forces into the atmosphere vast quantities of burnt fuel, ie sulphur dioxide, and other waste pollutants so much that trees under flight paths are severely affected, this was noted soon after the increase in air traffic in the seventies and eighties.

The process of atmospheric destruction is now speeding up through the activities of Homo sapiens, many of the early atomic power stations are coming to the end of their production life and are breaking down; in doing so they pour radioactive material into the atmosphere in concentrations that plant and animal life (including H. sapiens) cannot tolerate. The high cost and nil return of decommissioning an atomic power station means that safety levels cannot be properly maintained. While such power stations are in use finance has to be found to ensure that radioactive contamination does not get into the atmosphere, because its effect on cell division in plants and animals (including H. sapiens) can be disastrous leading to the production of mutations and monstrosities. This has already happened in those parts of Russia, Britain and America where accidents have occurred. Finance for decommissioning is even more essential in this respect and has to be found during the plant's active life.

The vast rain forest areas of the earth are essential for the maintenance of a healthy environment and atmosphere. Besides producing vast quantities of oxygen, trees recycle huge amounts of water into the atmosphere in a year, a single fully grown hardwood tree can lift seventy tons or more out of the earth and dispel it through its leaves into the atmosphere. Anyone living in sight of forest land or a rainforest will be familiar with the mists hanging amongst trees in the early morning or after rain. This is a vast recycling contribution to the rain clouds so often needed by areas away from the forests. It also sets up air currents that make the weather patterns of the world. The rain of Western Europe often originates in the forest of South or North America. Once these forests are destroyed then the rainfall in Europe will diminish and the land will dry out and become desert like North Africa. This process has in fact already started and is contributing to the shortage of water in Europe.

The greatest contribution to the destruction of the atmosphere will come from the destruction of the earth's ozone layer, for ozone is a gas made up of oxygen that occupies the upper layers of the atmosphere and helps block off the cancer-forming ultra violet rays from the sun. The thinning of the ozone layer means more of the rays will reach the earth's surface and increase the heating up of the earth, this is now leading slowly to the greenhouse effect so much talked about. In terms of average lifespan of the individual Homo sapiens it is a relatively slow process, but in geological terms it is happening quite rapidly. In a few thousand years the earth's surface could become too warm to maintain the environment and life as it is known today, the globe's land areas will all become deserts, unable to sustain existing life forms. That will be the time when Homo sapiens has used up the finite resources of the earth and will himself be entirely extinct. Anyone who has spent seventy years or more working in the open air will recognise that this process is already well under way and has accelerated in the past two decades. Exposing uncovered human flesh to the sun today is a health hazard that should not be ignored, especially by those with fair or light skins.

The third essential for the function of plant and animal bodies is nutrients in the form of carbohydrates, proteins, fibre, minerals and vitamins. These are all produced from the sun's rays by the growth of plants through the action of the chlorophyll in their leaves. The plant root takes up moisture and minerals from the soil in which it is growing, these are transferred up the plant by the process of osmosis already described, moisture and warmth are essential for this to happen, each plant cell formed will contain carbohydrates and minerals and at certain stages of growth protein, the cell walls will contain fibre. In the natural cycle of events if a plant dies and falls back into the ground, these nutrients are returned to the soil as a form of humus, the organic particles essential for a living soil. If the plants are eaten by an animal then

14

they are used to sustain and grow that animal's body and the waste products are eventually returned to the soil to add to the humus.

In the cycle of reproduction plants store food in a variety of ways for their own use or to survive the hard winter periods. The methods used include fruits, berries, nuts, stems and roots and in some specialised cases, leaves. Animals living off these plants have learnt to seek and use these storage organs for their own nutrition. The tuber of the potato plant has probably contributed more to the development of Western civilisation as known today than any other plant form, except perhaps the seed of the common cereals, wheat, barley, and oats, while the seed of the cereal rice has had a similar effect on the development of the Eastern society. Most of the dishes eaten by Homo sapiens across the world come from the storage of food by plants; and even the meat and fish in their diet originates from them. Thus the maintenance of the earth's plant population is vital for the continued existence of all members of the animal kingdom on earth.

It is the balance of nutrients that come from plants that is essential for healthy animal life, and the nearer the plant is to its natural form the better it is for the animal's body. Even the process of cooking or the preparation for serving can lower the nutritional value of a food, especially in the key areas provided by minerals and vitamins. The quicker a food is prepared and consumed the less the loss of nutrients involved, hence fresh vegetables straight from a garden or allotment are healthier foods than those that have been days in transit. Markets and shops, and overcooking can devastate nutrients, as can the modern additives used to prolong shelf life in shops and supermarkets. It is essential that diets made up almost entirely of processed foods should be supplemented by essential vitamins and mineral doses.

Already two thirds or more of the world's population is not having an adequate diet to maintain the human body in a healthy active state. The greatest cause of this is the shortage of pure water in the area they live in, nor do they have financial resources to obtain such a water supply. The other cause is the foods available to them are not balanced and capable of giving them the nutrients their body requires, the present financial system operated by Homo sapiens does not allow them to purchase such foods from the areas where supplies exist. This failure to supply adequate daily nutrition to two thirds of the world's population is the greatest condemnation of the International monetary system, which is not designed or developed to serve world trade, but to give power to and make profits for those who possess the wealth invested in the system at present.

An average size adult human being requires approximately two thousand and five hundred calories of nutrition per day to maintain its body in an active healthy state. Multiply that calorie requirement by the world population and it is possible to produce a figure that would adequately feed it. It has been shown that existing land areas could feed the population if properly farmed and maintained for an indefinite period to come. But the present financial system does not encourage it to happen and hence two thirds of the population are underfed, and receive contaminated water supplies. This failure is central to the present need to alter the International monetary system, otherwise wars and mass migration will continue and the earth's environment be destroyed at an ever increasing rate.

The growth of the world population and the Industrial system to produce wealth creates a vast amount of effluent and waste that is now poisoning the earth and its entire population of plants and all the creatures that live on them. Before such growth took place the effluents were broken down by natural processes, but the vast use of fossil and nuclear fuels has stopped this natural process by poisoning the organisms that carry it out, making it necessary to use artificial means of purifying effluent. Some of these artificial means may use natural processes to speed up the breakdown, a properly constructed septic tank will deal with and break down human effluent for many years without any difficulty, as will the larger sewage plants used in some cities. The solid by-products of such installations can either be returned to the soil as humus or broken down further in digester plants into products that could be used as extremely beneficial compost to improve garden soils. Some chemical industrial wastes are not so easily broken down

and more expensive chemical and incinerator plants may have to be used. It is however essential that any industrial process must include in its cost of production, the cost of the total destruction of its wastes. If this raises the selling price and sends it out of business, then so be it as the preservation of the environment is now more important than the product it manufactures. This means a change to purer and more natural lifestyles especially for many in the Western world, or where the motorcar has become an essential to the way of life.

Another vital key to the preservation of the earth's environment, besides the elimination of effluent, is the urgent need to recycle all products used by human society. Combustion of any form must be vastly reduced and eliminated wherever possible and eventually the reliance on fossil fuels stopped. In time all energy required by Homo sapiens must come from natural renewable sources such as wind, water movement by gravity and tides, the internal heat of the earth must be harnessed, and by-products of the human way of life used and treated to produce gases and heat that will produce energy. This will require large investment into research and development but will still be infinitely less than that made into nuclear and fossil fuelled plants and generators at present being used. A combination of sources of energy already available to small and large communities, from the village to a city could do this to meet their needs, coupled with proper conservation. Digester plants breaking down human effluent and producing methane gas, plus wind generators, and gravity powered water wheels (where possible) could go a long way to achieving this.

All this requires vast financial resources that the present economic system could not possibly meet by its existing mode of wealth generation. There are not vast profits to be made by such changes and the present banking methods cannot possibly have the reserves to set such schemes up and maintain them indefinitely. It is essential therefore to introduce a world financial system that is available to all according to their essential needs enabling them to set up recycling systems that will maintain their environment and to continue to exist. This is the greatest change that Homo sapiens has to make to social and economic structures worldwide. A stable, scientifically based economic unit directly related to human everyday energy requirement and use is the only way forward to do this. The availability of the unit must be directly related to the population numbers in the countries taking part in the scheme.

3

How To Conserve The Essentials Of Existence

The most important piece of knowledge that Homo sapiens requires to continue his existence on earth, is what are the basic requirements of its environment. As already outlined in previous chapters, healthy soil for plants to grow is fundamental to the continuation of life on earth, therefore the makeup of a viable soil must be understood, and the soil once formed must be maintained at all costs. There are many ways of preserving soil once formed but all require constant attention to details by the human involved. Neglect in one form or another quickly leads to the erosion and disappearance of that soil.

To grow a plant requires a healthy balanced soil which must contain all the basic components of soil. These are mineral particles, humus, nutrients, water and air in the right proportions for that plant. The mineral particles will come from bedrock and subsoil of the region in which the plant is growing, and the size of the particles will determine the nature of the soil. Small flat clay particles from aluminium based rocks will hold moisture easily while sandy soils from sandstones will have large particles that allow moisture to pass through quickly ie. free draining. In between these extremes are mixtures of clay and sand particles in varying proportions and the ideal soil (called loam) will have the right balance for most plant growth.

Humus is rotted and broken down organic matter, formed from plant and animal residues, these may have come from natural growth cycles or from the application to the soil of organic material by humans. A good growing loam will be rich in humus which improves the drainage of clay soils by separating out the small flat particles, or by filling in the spaces between sand particles and so slowing down the loss of moisture from that soil. It is possible to have too much humus in the soil, as in peat bogs or cold tundra areas where bacteria cannot work to break down the organic material because of too much moisture or too cold a temperature. It was the failure to maintain humus in the soil in the Midwest of

America earlier in the twentieth century that led to the wind erosion of the topsoil making the "Dustbowl" that drove settlers off their farms to migrate west to California. A balanced system of farming regularly replacing the humus content of the soil would have prevented this and led to the advocating of rotational cropping with grass following cereal crops and the keeping of livestock which came to be known as "Ley Farming". The binding together of soil by grass roots increases the humus content in a natural manner. Arable cropping, unless liberally treated with farmyard manure, depletes the humus content of the soil.

A plant obtains its nutrients from the mineral and humus content of the soil it is grown in. It is aided and abetted in this by soil bacteria that live in association with its roots. It is now known that some of the more prolific grasses used in farming today have up to and over one hundred different bacteria types attached to their roots helping them to take up their nutrients. If these are not present in the soil then the plant will not grow. The legume family (peas, beans, clovers, Lucerne etc.) are particularly important in this respect as the bacteria in the nodules on their roots fix nitrogen taken from the air by the leaves of the plant and deposit it in the soil, ready for the following crops; thus enriching the soil with the vital leaf forming nutrient at no extra cost to the farmer, so reducing the fertiliser bill and not using water polluting chemicals. It is unfortunate that to grow the huge quantities of food required by the ever increasing human population it has become essential to increase and maintain the soil nutrients by man made fertilisers. Excessive use of these has led to widespread pollution of water courses, lakes and seas and the subsequent destruction of wild life by such action.

Soil water, and soil air, are two essential components for the plant's well-being and the balance between them is crucial to produce healthy growth. Too much water in a soil leads to water logging and the exclusion of air. This in turn slows down the action of soil bacteria which will die if excessive water is not drained off. Peat bogs are an example of this in action, once drained and given time for the bacteria to act again then healthy growth will be restored. If there is too little water in a soil and an

excess of air instead, then the soil will heat too quickly, the process of osmosis by which plant takes up moisture and nutrients will slow down and cease, then the plant will quickly wilt and die. A plant will die from lack of water in about the same time as a human being, ie three days, if its roots are in an excessively dry soil. The management of air and moisture in the soil is crucial to successful cropping and is probably the greatest cause of desert formation at the present time. This is an area of environmental control on which man has to concentrate if he is to survive and maintain a basic standard of living. The constant film sequences by the media of dying and debilitating populations in drought stricken areas of the world are all too vivid illustrations in our homes of what happens when water is short in a soil.

Another fundamental for healthy plant growth is a stable atmosphere environment for it to grow in. A constantly warm temperature that gives the plant the chance to grow at a uniform rate is essential. Plants do not respond to wild fluctuations in temperature and it is essential to create a "micro" environment around the plant that is to its liking if the best results are to be obtained. Big variations between night and day temperatures must be avoided, as must exposure to either excessive amounts of wind or sunshine which speeds up the loss of moisture from the leaves. The creation of the right environment for good plant growth is now sufficiently understood for man to give protection to a plant from harmful effects to its growing atmosphere. In many cases it does not require over expensive provisions to make such conditions available. The well calculated planting of protection belts, hedges etc. can vastly alter the nature of a landscape and increase the number of plants that can be grown in it. It is where arid or desert conditions already exist that capital expenditure might become too much under the present financial system to be deemed uneconomic. The new financial system to be outlined later will make the cheap financial aid available to improve the environment in this way, and so reverse the present rapid loss of the right conditions for plant growth.

An early Victorian definition of a civilised man as "he who could change a bog or morass into an orderly garden", ignored the destruction of the natural fauna and flora that grows in that bog or morass. It also required a vast physical and financial investment in that area to achieve such a result, to say nothing of the continual effort required to maintain that orderly garden once it was created. The ever growing population of Homo sapiens means that more and more land with suitable topsoil must be cultivated and preserved for the survival of the species, this means soil conservation must become top priority in human activities and finance must be available to do this. Profits from crops grown in the topsoil under the present system will never be great enough to meet the expenses involved in soil conservation. Constant human effort on each area of soil will be required to stop erosion and maintain soil fertility. Water flow through the soil will have to be controlled and the ancient art of spreading water across land by leat or even terracing of hillsides resorted to.

There is evidence that the Chinese were using leats and canals to transfer water away from rivers well before the advent of Christianity. These used water held by natural obstacles such as gorges, waterfalls and lakes gently to take water along contours to irrigate places well away from rivers. They later introduced manmade weirs to hold back water so that this could be done. The irrigation systems needed to grow abundant crops were based on these canals and leats, and water was always available to produce heavy crops. With the continual drying of the earth's surface it is imperative that such water supplies by surface channel be set up wherever the soil is good enough to grow crops to feed humans or animals.

Leats were used much later in history to carry water to wheels designed to use the weight of the water passing over them to rotate and provide power to work millstones to grind corn. Some of these were still working in Europe and elsewhere till well into this century when fossil fuels replaced water as a source of power to fuel engines or generators that drove the mills. Canals big enough for the passage of cargo carrying boats were developed in the late middle ages, and their use continued to increase until the advent of the railways and later, road transport. But in many countries the systems still exist, some in working order, others in

varying states of dereliction. All these must be resurrected and brought back into use as a means of moving adequate irrigation water into the countryside, as a cheap way of transferring goods, and as a leisure resource, which has developed in the last few decades.

The introduction of canals and leats is especially important in semi-arid or desert areas where adequate water supplies in the soil will be needed for long periods of time, possibly decades. These are essential to rehabilitate that soil into a living mass that will carry plant life and even eventually produce adequate food crops. Canals must be used to transfer water from areas of a country with adequate rainfall to those that do not receive enough to maintain their basic soil in a living fertile condition. To achieve this will take years of work and need continual supplies of money to maintain the system. Once set up they must not be neglected and must receive constant attention from humans to maintain them. The present world economic system is totally incapable of financing such a scheme as the returns will not produce profits, or be capable of paying interest on the investments needed. But such a system properly set up with trained staff keeping it running could be a continual source of employment and produce food for vast numbers of the growing world population. Such a system could not be automated but would require individual human supervision to function, even a few hours of neglect could be disastrous to large areas of land.

The canal method of water distribution could best be installed in flatter areas of land, in hilly and mountainous regions another way of soil maintenance and conservation must be resorted to. This is the art or method of terracing fields, long known to man as is evident in many parts of the world. It involves the building of walls around the contours on the hill and mountain sides to keep back the topsoil in level strips, so that when cultivated and sown they do not wash away down the slope in heavy rain or when irrigated. The Incas used the technique in the Andes and there is plenty of evidence of it going back to very early times in many mountainous areas of the world, and exists today in many places. It requires a great deal of human effort to set up and maintain and would be a continual source of employment for the local population. The preserving of a healthy topsoil across the world must become an essential way of life and the economic system must be designed to do this without incurring vast debts and high interest payments.

Water supplies for irrigation to terraced areas will have to come from reservoirs higher up the mountains or pumped up from the river valley by pumps driven by wind, water or electricity. Gravity fed schemes from higher reservoirs will obviously be cheaper to install and maintain, and many of the early landscaped gardens across the world incorporated such a method. The principle goes back to the pre Roman times and was much copied by the great landscape gardeners of the eighteenth and nineteenth centuries. Such schemes should not use high technology but be simple to run and maintain using trained staff, not expensive technology, so creating purposeful employment.

Another aspect of soil conservation is the use of shelter belts of trees and shrubs, and suitably placed hedges to break the force of prevailing winds. Most of the deserts of the world were originally forests or woodland which were attacked by other species for food and more recently by man seeking fuel to warm himself and to cook by. The denuding of the forest led to the drying out of the topsoil and then rain and wind quickly started the process of erosion removing humus and goodness out of the soil and the desert was formed. With the cutting down of the rainforests this process in the tropical areas of the world and in the more temperate zones by the huge human requirements for softwoods is doing exactly the same thing. This process of topsoil loss could be slowed down if the stupid humans involved would cut in small patches, leaving mature shelter belts round them to contain the soil, stop drying out of the topsoil and to prevent wind and rain erosion. In the Middle Ages when this cutting down of trees and clearing of land was going on in Europe and later in North America the slow process of human energy being the only cutting power available, delayed the soil loss but the advent of the internal combustion engine and the chain saw to cut wood has altered all this and the loss of topsoil will accelerate in the next half century.

The removal of hedges in Britain and other parts of Europe have, in the last half century, led to the rapid loss of soil fertility over vast areas of land. If hedges and tree belts had been maintained then at least some of this fertility would have been preserved. The vastly increased use of fertilisers and pesticides that fertility loss has brought about could have been reduced by retaining chemicals in the soil and insect predators in the hedges and tree belts, so reducing some of the pollution of the soil water, streams, rivers and lakes. In the hillier and wetter areas of Britain, where hedgerows have been preserved, fertility loss has not been so marked though water erosion has increased where woodlands on slopes have been cut and sold but not replanted. In the modern desire to cash in on woodland crops, there are at present no incentives to make the owners replant those areas. This is contributing to the loss of topsoil.

Another essential of existence, the atmosphere, would also be helped by the planting of tree belts and hedgerows, for these would increase the production of oxygen into the atmosphere and counteract the growing amount of carbon dioxide in the air. It is often forgotten, in talking about the loss of the ozone layer that it is oxygen that is being lost, and plant life is the only source of replacement that Homo sapiens has, the cutting down of vast areas of rain and temperate forest contributes to this oxygen loss and so to the loss of ozone layer. To maintain a viable atmosphere means the reduction of combustion in all forms to stop carbon dioxide production, and to increase the plant population to step up the production of oxygen. The chemicals that destroy the ozone layer must at the same time be banned and severe penalties imposed to make their use uneconomical at all times.

The more civilised that Homo sapiens has become, the more they have been entrapped by the demands of the financial system to exploit the earth's environment and in so doing to destroy it. Other species have done this to a lesser degree when their numbers have outgrown their environment that supports them. But other species have had the sense to drive out their excessive numbers into untapped environments that could support the excess, or they have died through lack of nutrition. This is plainly seen happening in the former Yugoslavia at the present time and now Rwanda. Homo sapiens by its scientific and technical developments has greatly accelerated the process of destruction and already in parts of Asia, the Middle East and now in Europe deliberate genocide is being practised by nations to protect tracts of land against the demands of overpopulation so that those in power (mainly by superior weapons) can survive. It is always the fear that mass migration from less wealthy areas will swamp their own particular system of existence that drives a national group to do this. A basic inbred instinct of all species on earth is to protect their own particular territory and way of life. The better that lifestyle is, the more others in less fortunate positions will seek to achieve, usually by migration.

Because the earth, its crust and atmosphere are finite resources, Homo sapiens has got to use its intelligence to provide and conserve the essentials for all. This means the granting of equal basic status to all, male or female, irrespective of religious beliefs and national customs. The United Nations of the world must become the controlling force to do this with greatly increased powers over finance, regulatory powers and enforcement methods to ensure that eventually all nations work together to conserve the earth and its atmosphere. Every member of the human race must have access to the basic essentials of life; food, clean water, basic housing that suits the climate of their area, adequate drainage and waste disposal systems that do not pollute their living area, an up to date and properly resourced medical service, and a basic and advanced education service that enables them to develop their potential to serve the earth and the human race and other living species.

All nations have got quickly to accept that the present world economic system cannot supply the finance and wealth to carry such a basic scheme out. Well over two thirds of the world population are living in poverty and without access to most of the basic essentials of life listed above, and without any hope of raising their standards to those achieved in the so called "western world". To achieve such basic standards a fundamental change in financing the world must be introduced to conserve the environmental resources and use the inherent fundamental skills of the human mind and body to create wealth. This must employ every human being in work according to their ability and give them the previously listed basic standard of living. The energy to do this must come from the population of each national group using their skills and ability, and not destroying the resources of the earth, including the fossil fuels. Only in this way can the conservation of the earth be guaranteed for future generations.

The demands of the manufacturing and commercial systems must be secondary to the provision of basic essentials for human society. They should facilitate and provide the tools and services needed to organise the new financial order. The unnecessary luxuries that dominate the world markets must, for a long period, be eliminated so all can concentrate on bringing up the basic standards worldwide. The present world recession is already leading to a cutback in the production of such luxuries as the diminishing demand does not justify their production. It is essential that this situation continues until the inequalities in the financial system are eliminated and all have the basic standard of life. This will inevitably mean a reduction in living standards for many, but a raising of standards for the majority across the world population. It must become the function of a greatly enhanced United Nations to see this happen and enforce through the new financial system. All this will need a great deal of time and effort and the changing of many rigid attitudes, especially amongst politicians and financiers.

– 4 –
The Present World Economy Versus The Environment

The existing world banking system depends on the creation of wealth by Human Beings exploiting the assets of the earth to create goods and services for which they will be paid, or by lending the wealth they hold and charging the borrowers for the use of it. The scarcer the wealth in the banking system becomes, the higher the charge for borrowing it, and the increasing necessity to exploit the assets of the earth to a greater extent to provide extra wealth, the latter method has, in recent times, come to be called "growth in the economy". At no time and in no way does the economic wealth have any relationship to human needs or to the fact that it is the efforts of individuals or communities of individuals that created that wealth.

Any individual bank's wealth comes from the assets that its account holders are prepared to invest in it. In theory the bank should only lend out a fixed proportion of those assets, but in recent times this has been ignored and some major banking Institutions have become bankrupt because their borrowers have failed to repay their loans and as a result investors have lost their money.

The creation of wealth by exploiting the raw resources, be it vegetable, mineral or animal was developed by Homo sapiens from early times, especially in the Western world; they first organised the assets of their own country at the beginning of the Industrial Revolution period. Then, as demands grew, they went to undeveloped countries and set up colonies to exploit other countries' assets and the skill of their people. In the case of developing the vast American Continents that were mainly unpopulated, they actually exported their fellow human beings from their homelands in Africa to America, to work and develop the country's assets. Thus the vast slave trade developed depleting areas of Africa to create wealth in America. The use of slaves to create wealth has been one of the least attractive sides of the existing world banking system. It is still going on in parts of the world and the industrial development of the third world countries with low labour costs and low standards of living is really a thinly disguised form of slave labour where a worker in the third world, doing the same skilled job as a worker in the western world, is paid nothing like the same rate for the job.

What has been central to wealth creation to date is a seemingly infinite supply of resources from the earth to be exploited and a skilled labour force to develop those resources; but now in the second half of the twentieth century a drastic change has occurred in the relations between the earth's assets and the human population. The rapidly increasing and unchecked growth of the population across the world, and the finite supply of resources to be developed on the earth to meet demands of that population, means that wealth in the existing sense of the word, can no longer be created. Thus the supply of it, per head of the population is rapidly decreasing. This is happening at a time when Homo sapiens, educated by the modern media system is increasingly demanding a greater share of the developed assets of the world and the wealth of the banking system. This has been accelerated by the break-up of the Communist World of Eastern Europe and the changeover to free trade in Communist China. In no way will the existing banking organisations have enough assets to meet the requirements of such an ever growing increase in demand.

The immediate result of this, coupled with the advances in technology that do not require human beings to operate them, is a rapidly growing proportion of the population who cannot find employment to earn money to acquire the basic essentials of life and so they experience the miseries that stem from that situation. Thus annually the numbers migrating from poorer to wealthier areas of the world is growing, and is now even happening between the wealthier nations. Germany, because of its so-called wealth, is becoming a honeypot to migrants in a way that America did earlier in the twentieth century. These catastrophic migrations take place because the International banking Organisations do not provide enough currency and credit to each individual country to buy its populations basic requirements of food, clean water, basic housing, adequate drainage, medical services, and an adequate education service. It is the daily manifestation on the media screens, of the growing failure of the world economic system. Growth in the system cannot possibly meet demand. This is at a time when the countries of Europe are encouraging people to cut back production especially of food and other essential products in an effort to stabilise world trade. This is another example of the stupidity of Homo sapiens. The demand is only too obvious for all to see, but the economic systems are incapable of meeting that demand.

To achieve growth in the modern meaning of the economic world means even more of the finite resources of the earth must be developed and destroyed. The expanding use of fossil fuels illustrates this probably more than anything else, for these are capable of being used up within the lifetime of children already born into this world. The total oil supply could be exhausted by the middle of the twenty-first century, the known gas supply even sooner than that, while coal could last to the end of the next century, its increased use would speed up the destruction of the atmosphere unless much cleaner methods of burning it are developed. The raw materials of basic metal production are also in limited supply if demand is greatly increased. Here recycling of existing supplies is a possibility and is on the increase already but in the light of population increase a far greater effort will have to be made to stop the exhaustion of the earth's existing supplies of all raw materials used by man.

The most vital environmental resource being destroyed by economic demand is probably Timber. Since the beginning of time the symbiotic relationship between Homo sapiens and the world's forests has been ignored by the economic systems. Over two thousand years ago one of the great Greek philosophers wrote "cut down a forest to create a city and you soon have a desert." Homo sapiens, the naked ape, cut down trees for warmth, then for cooking, then for building homes and ships, and now for the production of paper and packing material. The vast forests of northern Canada, Russia and China have long been disappearing as are the world's rainforests. It is estimated that by the year 2030 all the world's prime forests will have been cut down. This is the result of the operation of the economics of madness, to every tree cut down, three should be planted – one that will die from attacks by animals, pests and disease, the second will grow to be cut as a young sapling timber to meet demands for such timbers, and so allow the third to mature into an adult tree, flowering and producing seed, oxygen and moisture into the atmosphere and eventually mature timber for man's use. All this will require a great deal of human effort (employment) and space, in competition with Agriculture, services such as towns and cities, railways, reservoirs, roads, airfields etc.

Because of the rapid increase of population and the pollution of the earth's surface that stems from it, water, the most essential environmental resource of all has now become an asset to the world economic systems. In Western Europe and elsewhere clean water supplies are now becoming more and more expensive, and as the standard of living is raised across the earth this cost will grow. Within the next few decades clean water will be more expensive than petrol, diesel and gas, and the conservation of clean water is central to the survival of Homo sapiens. This is the key environmental problem that must not become a wealth creating idea for the economic systems. All human and other life on earth has a fundamental right to water, and no one from a banking system to the most dictatorial ruler has a mandate to withhold it. The basic humanitarian rights under the United Nations Charter must be first of all clean water, and an adequate food supply for every man, woman and child on earth, and no banking system must prevent that happening. A Chinese philosopher said a very long time ago that water is the blood of the earth and all life depends on it.

It can be seen from the issues raised above that the present world economy, reliant on growth from developing the earth's resources, cannot work hand in glove with the urgent necessity to preserve and improve the environment. The fundamental basis on which it has developed and is attempting to continue is flawed. It advances credit to those who want to cut down the world's forests, it encourages the cornering and charging for clean water supplies and most foolishly of all it encourages human beings society's greatest asset, to be unemployed and idle, destroying their self respect and making them feel outcasts from human society. Hence the vast increase in world crime (the poor and deprived robbing the rich to live), and local wars, as seen in the Balkans and elsewhere caused by local essential assets being denied to some; and also the migrations that are pressurising the wealthier nations. Germany's economy, strong as it is, will not be able to bear the luxury of reunification and a mass inflow of migrants in this decade or in the foreseeable future.

The rapidly growing instability in the world's political systems, especially in Europe, the Americas and the former countries of the Soviet Union is a direct outcome of the rapid breaking down of the International monetary system. Only in China, where the oppressive Communist regime controls the mass of the people, denying them their human rights under the United Nations Charter, does some semblance of stability appear to remain. But here again the influence of the world media and the education of the Chinese people by it, will eventually lead to a breakdown of stability and the overthrow of the oppressive regime. Over a quarter of the world's population is on the Chinese mainland, a people who are extremely self disciplined and hard working and will, with their vast natural resources, outstrip and outlast the rest of the world; until they too use up their natural resources. Already the Yangtze River is flooding excessively and is heavily polluted by cities along it. The remaining wild population of the Panda species is severely threatened by Homo sapiens intruding their territories. The Chinese Government are appealing for world help for finance to prevent this happening. The control of the human population in that region is really the only way this can be done.

It is a strange quirk in the makeup of human intelligence that it insists on standards being fixed and acceptable to all as regards requirements, temperature, volume, length, weight, area; and through religions; standards of behaviour, but, it does not seem to want a fixed, immovable standard for the value of the world's monetary units! Money markets, banking, financiers, the Mafia and the drug barons would fight this to the last man, because it would remove one valuable source of wealth acquirement if there was a fixed, accepted standard of a monetary unit. The ever present disarray in the world's money markets, the GATT negotiations, and between nations of the European Community is because somebody has been audacious enough to propose a common unit of exchange in Europe. The value of that unit is not to be scientifically fixed like all other standards, but float according to the market demands, thus making a nonsense of the unit from the start. Even if it was adopted in Europe it would still enable the young men in the money markets across the world to go on playing their computer games and determine the price of the Unit, thus creating inflation or devaluation when it suits them.

If Homo sapiens is going to survive as a species on earth for another thousand years then it has collectively across the globe to accept that it is just another animal species who must live in harmony with other species and the global environment. Because of its overdeveloped intelligence, its demand on the environment is much greater than other species, and so finds it necessary to have financial units of exchange to enable it to produce necessities (and luxuries) and to trade with one another. An unbiased, detailed analysis of the financial system, and what actually creates wealth will show the enquiring mind that there is only one real unit of production, and that is of the human being in its immediate environment, or collectively in the environs of the community. Human society today is made up of a vast collection of communities of all colours, tongues and religions across the surface of the earth. In setting up the United Nations after the second World war, a basic attempt was made to unify and control the behaviour of those communities so that all could live in peace and prosper, with equal rights, irrespective of sex or religion across the globe.

This was a vital concept, written into the United Nations Charter after the Second World War, fifty years later it still has not been achieved and the main reason why is the inequality brought about by the financial systems operating across the globe. Human beings still have different values in different areas of the world, and the value of similar goods produced by human effort in one part of the world is different from that in other areas. To a large extent this has led to the long lasting depression of Western home markets' economies because they cannot compete with the ever growing flow of cheap goods from the Third World countries produced at a much lower price than that with which their workers, with their higher living standards, can compete. The industrialisation of the poorer areas of the globe where labour is cheaper and living standards much lower is a situation that cannot last much longer when mass education (by the media) makes them demand higher standards of living and higher wages to provide that improvement. It also means the population of the poorer areas are demanding the right to destroy their natural environment in order to sell its products to the richer areas, to raise money to meet the ever increasing demands of their people; thus accelerating global destruction, especially the oxygen producing forests.

The two world wars in the Twentieth century because of their vast destruction of the environmental and financial assets of the world financial system, accelerated the using of the earth's resources and led twice to chaos in the world's monetary system. The recession and then depression after World War One and now after World War Two burnt up the Banking Wealth across the globe. After the first world war the Gold Standard, the first basis of world trade, was abandoned because a majority of nations had used up their gold reserves. After the second world war when there was no gold standard, aid from the Western World had to be used (once again) to establish stability and trade in the world markets. The situation was so desperate in the nineteen-fifties, a new form of wealth creation was resorted to, a kind of cannibalisation that not only destroyed the globe's resources but also the resources of the financial system. This has come to be known as "Asset stripping" whereby a company is bought out by another company and its assets are sold off to create more wealth for the purchasing company. The individual skills and work teams that made up the original company are ignored and the productive potential of those teams is lost to human society.

Since the nineteen-fifties this process has accelerated and is now, in Great Britain, an active and central part of Government policy. This time it is called "privatisation", where the material assets and superstructure, gas, electricity, telephones, health service, water and soon railways and coal, will be sold to private individuals to create short term wealth for the government of the day. Thus the nation's environmental resources are sacrificed to meet the day to day running of the nation. The needs of the human society for these facilities are totally ignored and eventually only those who can afford them will be able to have them. The economic system now dictates what humans shall or shall not have, it no longer meets the needs of, or supplies necessities of life to that individual, unless they are lucky enough to be employed and earning enough to meet their daily needs. No amount of growth, or the using up of the earth's resources will overcome the cracks and flaws in this economic system. If continued it must inevitably mean the destruction of the species Homo sapiens. It is similar to the old story of the dinosaur's nervous system being so primitive that they could eat their own tails without feeling or knowing what they were doing. In an effort to balance the national day to day budget, this nation, and others in the world are steadily eating their own bodies.

Across Britain and elsewhere in the world, social and financial resources are destroyed because the banking and commercial organisations are fighting to preserve themselves, the disappearance of the corner shop in suburbs because a supermarket opened on the edge of town, the village shop and post office is closing down because supermarkets in local towns undercut them to attract trade and provide free transport to fetch in the customers. Smaller garages struggle to continue and bigger ones have to raise their labour costs to stay in business; thus decreasing the use motorists make of them because their costs are too high. In the mad world of the European Community Agricultural Policy, farmers who can easily increase milk production are put on quotas to avoid a "milk mountain", yet the Third World which could absorb milk powder for their undernourished children, cannot buy the surplus because they are short of available currency to do so. Already across the world and in Britain individuals are grouping together to set up Local exchange Trading Schemes or "Lets" with locally agreed currencies with which they pay one another for services because of lack of national currency in their pockets. Car mechanics are carrying out servicing work for a haircut, typists are turning out neatly produced documents for which they are paid with a night's babysitting. The largest network is around Stroud in Gloucestershire, others are in Brighton, Manchester, Lewes, Haverfordwest and Totnes, Devon where acorns are the unit of exchange – perhaps appropriate for an area that can produce such good oak trees, it is said that in Totnes one is unorthodox if one appears in a collar and tie!

Economists and politicians have forgotten nowadays a basic law that used to be taught to students of Agricultural economics; the Law of Diminishing Returns stating simply that one can increase production to a certain level when it will peak and then start to diminish, no matter how much effort or resources are put into it. Agricultural scientists have increased production by use of genetics, improved fertilisers, fungicides and pesticides, but they are now losing the battle of demand from a growing population because of the law of diminishing returns and the outcry from Environmentalists about the destruction of the environment which has been brought about through their own behaviour. A lower output from an organically balanced system of production will have to be the way forward to meet growing demands using more, not less land, making the European Community policy of "set aside" a complete nonsense at this time of economic and environmental disaster. The only correct answer lies in increasing production by organically balanced methods and a global economic and monetary system that facilitates the free flow of goods and materials from where they can easily be produced, to areas of high demand that cannot meet their local demands from their own resources. People that have, or can obtain by trade, the basics of life in their own area are unlikely to consider migrating to other areas, because the basic wealth of such areas would be available readily to them.

The world monetary system can no longer produce enough wealth to sustain the human population, yet it continues to increase the number of them without work; there is a continued growth of the unemployed across the globe. Nothing of value to human society is produced without activity on the part of a human being. Because of their physical and mental makeup they can only work a certain number of hours per day, the rest of the day is spent relaxing, socialising and sleeping. To do this they require a level of nutrition that will maintain their body in good health and provide them energy to work, play and sleep according to each individual's body requirements, usually related to size and structure but varying from individual to individual. It has long been possible to measure the amount of heat required by the average body to do this daily feat of nutrition. namely two thousand five hundred Calories. This daily requirement should be the unit of finance used in the world, by this fixed basis all other activities could be measured and related. Today units of energy are measured in Joules and a Joule equals 4.1868 calories, thus it would be possible, if the unit of finance is based on calories, for the cost of production to be calculated on a scientific basis.

- 5 -

The Way To Change The World's Economic Structure

The new monetary system based on the daily requirement of the human body in energy terms, must make a continuous supply of these units available to all countries and areas of the world on equal terms. It is suggested that the name of the unit be SAP, chosen because sapiens in Homo sapiens, means wise, abbreviate that to SAP and that means any vital body fluid for life in plants or animals, providing energy and vigour. Therefore the basis of the new world financial system is a SAP which equals two thousand and five hundred Calories, or five hundred and ninety seven point one Joules, (597.11). It should be administered and distributed by the United Nations Organisation and be freely available to all people who live in Democracies who elect their Governments by Proportional Representation, preferably the single transferable vote method (STV). This would ensure that every political viewpoint would be represented in a country's government and all the population over the age of eighteen, male and female, would have a vote. This control of the system would give the United Nations the power to insist on the Charter of Human Rights being operated in the countries that qualify to participate and also that they would be properly and adequately financed to provide the human rights.

The daily credit available under the system should be sufficient to supply each participating country and area's needs for food, clean water, basic housing to suit the climate of the area and the power supplies to service that housing; adequate drainage and waste disposal systems that do not pollute the environment; up to date and properly resourced medical services and basic and advanced education services to train the population to run and maintain the structure of the environment. This would be called the basic or first tier of the economic system and no interest will be paid on the money (SAPs) made available, merely the administrative costs to the UN would have to be met, thus eliminating the drain of high interest charges that are at present crippling world banking and finance. The credit daily on this tier would be based on the certified population number in each country and area. The second or commercial tier of the new system would be the existing banking and finance activities, available to individuals, with fixed interest charges that would not fluctuate, enabling them to continue to provide the other necessities for modern life. This second tier would greatly benefit from the finance made available to the first tier, the flow of currency (SAPs) that would stem from the basic provisions would make revenue and capital available to the second tier.

Control of the financial system by the United Nations is vital to stop any particular section of the world community from gaining control of the system. Each country qualifying and participating should have an equal vote in the decision making. No veto system should be allowed to operate, as at present in the Security Council, in relation to the financial system. Countries, and separate areas of countries should be able to make their claims for finance for the first tier on the basis of individual rights to maintain their environment and their population. By making the essential key for qualification the election of the national and local government by Proportional Representation, it will ensure all groups, ethnic or political, have a say in what money is spent on, and the provision is fair to all. This will ensure that Dictators or one party Governments do not qualify for finance under the scheme. Some of the major countries of the world would not qualify at present and would need to revise their electoral system. The United Nations would need to monitor the electoral system in each country and how the elections are conducted. It would also need to set up national and area offices to run the credit system and vet submissions for essential finance. In all cases the submissions would have to include and meet fundamental environmental standards to protect and enhance the local environment and ensure no pollution occurred.

Finance would automatically be available under the scheme to qualifying areas to meet food, water, housing, drainage, medical services and education needs based on population numbers. Thus a nation of fifty million producing little or none of its own food;

only thirty percent of its housing with clean piped water; outdated drainage, and waste disposal polluting the air, water supply, and the nearby seas; little or no medical services or education structure, would immediately qualify for vast credit to start to rectify its needs. Finance to buy food on the world markets would be top priority, then the nation could submit costed schemes to provide adequate water; housing for seventy percent of its population; modern waste disposal and drainage plants, hospital and clinics; schools, and teachers for them. This would be a vast undertaking and take many years to achieve but it would provide work for all in the nation. It would stop inter area wars as seen today on the media, and the continual pictures of dehydrated bodies through lack of nutrition in a world that has the knowledge and ability to produce adequate food supplies, because they would have the finance to meet their population demands. In time, and after a lot of hard work they would have also water, housing, an energy supply, drainage and waste systems, medical schemes and an education for all according to their ability. It will not have denuded the world of vital and essential mineral, vegetable or animal resources because schemes approved, and financed will have to protect and enhance these as they progress.

The national submission to the United Nations by the country in the example above, should include plans for each of its regions and areas, as put forward by those regions or areas and brought together in a national overall plan. This is where the vital part that Proportional Representation in elections comes into play, especially in those countries where ethnic or minority groups exist, such as the former Yugoslavia, or the Baltic States of the former USSR. Where good agricultural land exists and food for its own population can be grown, then the basic allowance of the credit to buy food could be used to supplement provisions of other essential needs, where their standards are not up to the Charter of Human Rights. For example, once Britain changed its electoral system to qualify for the new International Finance system, then Agricultural production could be increased again and the credit given for buying food could be used to house the homeless, provide care and pensions for the elderly and reopen many of the hospital beds at present closed because of shortage of funds. The costing of the schemes would have to use SAP units as their basis and they would be submitted and discussed with the regional and national office of the U.N. set up to deal with them in that country. Submissions made for financial credit, based on population numbers, would have to be in two parts as is operative in present schemes for financial help, both for capital outlay and day to day revenue to carry out the capital programme, and then to finance the running of the expanded scheme in future years. This would immediately create a great deal of activity, which does not take place at present because of shortage of finance. There should be schemes to train the necessary skilled labour in all areas of need, food production, transport and distribution, production of materials, building of housing, hospitals, schools etc. In many countries of the Third World the provision of a clean and adequate water supply would be a mammoth task, requiring vast capital expenditure on desalination and purification plants, major distribution pipelines, reservoirs to hold the water stocks, then local distribution pipelines to the new adequate housing for the population. This alone would create years of meaningful work for the local population, once trained to do the work, and in those countries that supply the necessary goods and equipment, such as pipes, plant, fittings, excavation machinery etc. In many areas it would probably take half a century to achieve, and then it has to be adequately maintained. If it was left to the present banking organisations they could not produce the reserves of cash to do it, and the interest they would charge would, as it does now, stop the country from applying anyway. Where such schemes are already in operation revenue expenditure will have to be financed internationally, based on population numbers to keep the system maintained, running and updated as necessary. The production and resources of the receiving nation will always be inadequate to meet their needs, the present depression in the finances of the Western World is a direct outcome of the nations being unable to produce adequate revenue to maintain their internal structure.

Before this SAP financial scheme is set up, standards of provision under the scheme will have to be laid down and agreed by all participating nations and areas. This will inevitably be a slow process, though many of the more developed countries already have agreed standards but cannot achieve them because of lack of finance. The shortage of money to go ahead will be overcome by the SAP scheme and the low standards of provision in many of the poorer areas will automatically be raised to meet those laid down by the United Nations. It will be inevitable that the poorer, backward, nations will have to be allowed much more financial backing than prosperous Industrial ones that already have high standards of housing, water supplies etc. in their social structure. The latter group of nations will prosper from the trade generated in supplying capital goods and "know-how" to the developing countries. In time the backward nations will become much more self-supporting and able to run their own social structure without trading so much with the developed ones of the world, but they will not, as at present, want to become industrialised to produce excessive wealth to obtain the basic necessities as they have to now. The schemes they put forward to obtain credit under the SAP system should be aimed at providing the social structure without destroying, but actually improving, and enhancing both their own and the overall global environment – such as replanting rain and temperate forests and conserving and recycling water supplies. If the implementation of this SAP system is tackled vigorously and all nations and areas eventually qualify to participate through changing their electoral system, it could have achieved its objective, that the Charter of Human Rights be available to the whole world within a century. If this is not done the future of the species Homo sapiens is in doubt, as the atmosphere and global environment deteriorates through lack of sufficient water and oxygen to sustain existing life.

A pattern of priorities in each participating country and area will have to be agreed to ensure that human effort is directed into those requirements having the highest priority. Proper provision of food and water to all in both cities, towns and rural areas must be met first for these are the essentials of life, energy and vigour to carry out the other essential priorities. Power installations and housing, including the making of the building materials must be the next in order of priorities. Power installations must be based on renewable energy supplies such as wind, water and tide, while housing must be suitable for the climate of an area. The standards of housing in a district may vary according to altitude, exposure and local climatic patterns. At the same time as the power and housing are developed, so must the drainage and waste disposal system to cope with the environment problems coming from improved housing standards. Proper sewage systems incorporating digester plants must be built so no sewage or effluent is released into the river systems. This is one area in the Western world that will need a considerable amount of work to be done. As the food, water and housing is improved then the medical and education services must be developed to meet the standards laid down, this will not of course involve a considerable building programme in all districts. The mistakes at present being made in the British Health Service must be avoided where big central (or not always so central) Hospitals are being developed to cut management costs, at the expense of patient care. Patient care in small local hospitals and clinics, where local people have easy access and are familiar with the staff and set up, adequately financed to run in such a manner must be the top priority, especially in the more isolated country areas. Schools must also be small and suited to the requirements of the local communities and environment demands, with further education facilities being on the same campus, against the large centralised system that at present is favoured in Britain. Small and properly financed is beautiful in the fight to maintain and improve the local and national environments, and so health of the Global Atmosphere.

Once the basic social structure is in place, and unemployment eliminated, then the daily credit and finance can be turned to the development of the commercial tier in the system and less essential or more luxurious goods produced. Again this development must enhance and improve the environment, not destroy it. Sites of Special Scientific Interest (SSSIs) must have priority and not be destroyed because some stupid planner wants to cut a road through it just to keep costs down. Roads and factories must be screened off by suitably sited shrub banks and copses of trees to act as a shelter belt, and to enhance the atmosphere with oxygen production. Wherever possible luxuries such as cars, containers, sports equipment etc. should use materials that can be recycled and so cut down the use of scarce earth resources such as ironstone, limestone and other minerals, the supply of which is limited and costly to extract and transport to the centre of manufacture. By basing costings on energy use it will be apparent to manufacturers that recycling must make sense, compared with the extraction and processing of prime raw materials. Non essential goods should have no priority over the working of the basic social structure that preserve the local environment.

The second or commercial tier of the new finance system should, as now, be responsible for the day to day transactions of people's everyday lives. The existing banking structure will conduct this field of activity and will be expected to keep its interest rates as low as they can so as not to restrict activity by taking too much profit out of the system. The first tier of finance will relieve the existing banks of the requirements to provide massive loans for the food production, water capital works, housing, except to private individuals who want their own properties, ie. to invest their own earnings or private capital into property, drainage and waste disposal, and will not need massive loans from the banks for their maintenance and provisions as now. The same will also apply to health and education provision. The commercial banking tier will automatically benefit from the finance injected in the first tier projects, with wages, materials, transport, and the whole infrastructure having a greater supply of the financial units. The massive shortage of capital and revenue finance created by the existing system will be done away with until all basic human demands and environmental improvements have been met. World wide this could take a century or more to achieve and the commercial banking system will have to comply and meet the restrictions of the international system so that they help monitor the drastic improvement that will be necessary to save the earth's environment. Where excess profits are taken in commercial transaction, taxation must be applied to discourage such profiteers.

44

The changeover of the commercial and service tier of financing to using SAP units, should be undertaken as quickly as possible in those countries that qualify under the Electoral conditions laid down by the United Nations. Qualifying countries could, if they wish to, apply the name of their existing main currency to the SAP unit, providing its value is the same as the SAP. It will be quite easy to evolve a costing system for production and transactions based on energy use with the SAP central to that system. In this way high energy using methods will soon be obvious to all and this, in turn will lead to changes in methods used so that energy will be reduced and production costs lowered, thus ensuring that the environment is further protected. The commercial banking systems will quickly learn to use SAP units in both their customer's accounts and in their own internal methods. Because modern high 'tech' systems of accounting require a lot of energy to operate them, then older manual methods may well be found to be more efficient, as well as being more accountable to accurate audits. The present high rate of fraudulent dealing resulting from the use of high energy using machines will not be so easy if an increased number of human minds are involved, thus cutting down the losses of banking resources that now occur through criminal operators in the working of the machines.

Once a country qualifies and joins the International banking and credit system, then it will have to decide whether to use the SAP units instead of their present units; or, agree a valuation of the SAP in terms of their present unit. For instance, in Britain once it had changed its electoral system to proportional representation, it would have to decide if the pound was equal to one SAP. It would have fifty five million pounds plus a day available for its banking system to buy food, and more if its development schemes were approved and financed internationally. Or, if in Britain it was decided that to provide two thousand five hundred calories of food to each person at a cost of five pounds the SAP would equal five pounds not one. Because the value of the SAP is based on human requirements and is universally available, the present fluctuation in currency values is eliminated and stability is achieved in world food markets; requirement, not supply and demand will be the regulating factor. It does not matter what the SAP unit is called by a particular community as long as the basic valuation is accepted by all trading with that community. The present groups of young men playing their computer games in the world's money markets can then be much more usefully employed in calculating unit costs in calories for specific production methods, not messing about upsetting world trade by fluctuating the various currency values.

There is a major task ahead of the young computer experts (male or female) in calculating SAPs, calories, or Joules, the value of each product, service or component used in the social system. These calculations will have to be done and published in all countries qualifying for the system before the whole scheme begins. Experts in various fields of activities will have to be involved in this so that accurate and agreed values can be included in the guide rules used in calculating costs of production, value of services rendered or operations carried out. In the Western world such guide books of calorific values already exist for foods so that those with a weight problem can calculate the number of calories a day they are consuming. For instance an apple produces 40 calories per oz. (28 grms.) per serving, brown bread loaves produce 60 calories per oz. whereas dried bread crumbs produce 100 calories per oz. Animal fats such as butter produce 205 calories per oz. (28 grms.). Fried cooked foods are notoriously rich in calories, a hamburger will produce 260 to 320 calories per oz. according to who makes it! The popular Kentucky Fried chicken produces 850 calories per oz. and every ounce of chipped potatoes eaten with it add another 70 calories per oz. so three ounces of chicken and three ounces of chips are more than sufficient to feed an average human being per day. Similar guide rules also exist for fuel and energy sources. It is a known and commonly used calculation just how many Joules a barrel of oil will produce, or a cubic metre of gas or a tonne of coal. In these cases the source and type of the product will affect the Joules produced.

Once such books of guide rules of calorific values are available under product headings or on floppy disks, then it will be possible to do all costings and pricings in calories and business structures will be assessed in the same SAP units. Materials, labour and capital costs can then be priced in calories and so in SAPs, the total cost of an operation, or its valuation for audit purposes will be in the same units, and comparisons will point out how energy saving can be achieved. This will be of particular value in cutting down the excess use of energy production methods that burn fossil fuels, and so further pollute the atmosphere because such fuels are notoriously bad in energy conversion into calories available to be used in human activity. In time this will encourage the changeover to renewable sources of energy and eventually eliminate the use of fossil fuels. Many operations that at present use high energy production methods that make the employment of human labour unnecessary could be eliminated, and useful employment of the growing world numbers of unemployed be introduced. It may well slow down the rate of production but more importantly it will also slow down the level of pollution and the destruction of the vital life giving atmosphere. High speed, high energy using production methods are already flooding the world with unwanted goods at the cost of the irreplaceable earth's resources.

If the United Nations Organisation is to introduce control and operate the financial system to ensure their Charter of Human rights is available to all, it is essential that the National and Local Governments in the participating countries are elected by proportional representation. For in this method the governing body will represent the views of all who voted in proper proportion of parties according to the votes cast for them. This will almost inevitably mean that most Governments in the system, will be Coalition ones of parties, for the ruling Cabinet must also contain representatives in accordance to the proportion of those who voted in favour of the parties. To qualify single party government must be eliminated so making the suppression of minorities a thing of the past. The U.N.O. will have to approve and monitor the elections in each country that joins the scheme, and those that fail to comply will be refused access to the first tier credit for essential social structure works. All voters must feel that their views are being heard and voiced at the centre of government. This is essential to eliminate the injustice felt at present that the majority of the world population do not have a say in the government of the day. The Italians, who recently voted to change from proportional representation to first pass the post, will soon find that the latter method can be even more corrupt than PR as their experience in the 1930s should have shown them under Mussolini where political expression was suppressed. In Britain, always quoted as the centre of democracy, since World War Two all governments have been elected on minority votes, and the election of 1992 returned a Conservative Government with fourteen million votes while twenty million voted against their policies. Hence the unrest widely felt in Britain after that election and towards its Government of the day.

The tables below show how unfair the present electoral system is compared with proportional representation and why the greater proportion of the population is dissatisfied with the present system of election:

Present System, 1992 Election Results in Britain

	% votes	Parliamentary Seats	% seats
Conservatives	42.0	336	52
Labour	35.4	271	42
Liberal Democrats	17.9	20	3
SNP/PC	2.5	7	3

under Proportional Representation using the Single Transferable Vote method, the result would have been:

	% votes	P.R. seats	% seats	Change in No. of seats
Conservative	42	275	42.2	-61
Labour	35.4	237	36.4	-34
Liberal Democrat	17.9	102	15.7	+82
SNP/PC	2.5	20	3.1	+13

thus under this system the views of the voters would be represented in proportion to the national vote: (source of information, The Electoral Reform Society.)

During the transition period to the new International Financial System many countries will not qualify for participation in the scheme. Dictators, Military Rulers and political parties that remain in power purely because they will not change their method of election, such as the Conservative Party in Britain, will deny their citizens the benefit and improvements to their social structure that will stem from the scheme, and the humanitarian controls that come from the United Nations overall supervision. They will obviously have to continue to borrow money to maintain their systems from the Commercial Banking Organisations of the second tier of finance, and while interest rates will be lower than at present, it will cost them much more than under the new scheme. To speed them into making the change financial pressure must be brought to bear on them to introduce the fair electoral system, and cut down on using diminishing earth's resources and eliminate much of the pollution their methods are causing. It will not be acceptable to have a great portion of the world's population trying to save the planet while an avaricious and wealth seeking section continue to speed up its destruction by their methods. Such pariah nations and areas must be quickly convinced of the need to convert to the earth friendly system.

Rapidly to introduce the new International Finance system will need detailed organisation of training of suitable staff across the globe and the production of supplies to meet the vastly increased demands that will speedily develop in all participating areas as the scheme gets under way. Staff to set up the control structure must be trained first, and then they in turn must organise and oversee the training of technical staff to produce the supplies locally where possible; or the shipment in of supplies that have to come from elsewhere in the world. This will stimulate employment and bring back into use many of the skills and technical ability that at present are being lost to society at large because of the world depression and failure of the existing economic systems. With the present rundown of the world's mercantile fleets across the globe and the rapidly ageing fleets that are operating, one of the first priorities will be a programme to build ships that are modern, safe and non-polluting, to transport essential supplies from areas that can produce, to those that have neither the materials nor the technical skills to produce supplies to meet their needs now they have currency to buy. This logistic programme will take many years to implement and carry out and will create a demand for labour that the present economic systems have no hope of ever creating.

Each participating country must set up an education and training system to produce Technicians and a skilled labour force to control and run the environmental protection schemes required of them for being members of the International Finance system. For the more advanced Nations such education systems already exist, but the countries that do not have them will need a lot of help from the United Nations in setting up schools, colleges and training centres to achieve this. The whole of a nation's population will need to be trained and then continually operate the environmental protection scheme that will be required of them. The avoidance of polluting the countryside, streams and rivers will require co-operation from everyone. The planting of trees and shrubs and their protection afterwards must be stamped on everyone's mind from an early age; small boys with big penknives must be taught to carve bits of wood and not cut down and vandalise young growing trees and shrubs as so often happens these days, while courting couples must stop mutilating the bark of established trees with the love signs of their affection. The education systems must continually make the population aware of the ever present and growing need to protect and control the local environs so that future generations will be able to live in a healthy, happy state, and not be debilitated by fumes, pollution and too little oxygen in the atmosphere they breathe, or poisoned by the water they drink and use in everyday living. Environmental protection must be taught to every child from a very early age and continued throughout their lives. The present mistakes in relation to the environment must be reversed and eliminated if the species Homo sapiens is to survive.

To run the financial support system in each participating country the United Nations Finance Section will need to set up Regional and local Offices to work closely with the local Council each country will have elected by P.R. It is envisaged that the countries will be divided into regions and each region will have an appropriate number of areas similar to the counties in Britain, each of which will have its own council made up of representatives of each party according to the votes cast for them, again ensuring all political and ethnic views are represented. In each of these areas the United Nations should have a local Office that will administer the finance support required, scrutinise and approve the plans for schemes of food supply, housing, power supply, drainage etc. Each region will then have a U.N. office to check that these local schemes are all part of the Regional and National schemes before financial support is given. This will protect against one local area or county making proposals that are detrimental to the environment of another, especially where pollution of another area could occur, or water supplies are directed away from neighbouring areas. This is already happening in the Balkans and parts of Central Europe, and in China and South America where hydro-electric schemes are being set up to the detriment of other regions. The staffs in such offices must contain a high proportion of nationalities other than the indigenous population to ensure the scheme is carried out without corruption or nepotism. Here again this structure would have to be in place very early in the setting up of the whole scheme in the participating country.

This regional and local structure of finance-giving Offices would have to work closely with the national and local banking systems of the second tier of commercial financing to ensure that duplication of credit does not take place. Because of the natural duplicity of some members of the species Homo sapiens, checks must be in place to see that individuals or groups of individuals do not draw finance from both systems to finance the same scheme. The giving of credit by the Commercial banking system must be more carefully scrutinised than many of the schemes in the 1980s when vast sums of money where loaned by the banking world for developments that were not required by society and were environmentally disastrous; many big cities across the globe bear monuments to this policy. The finance given by the U.N. schemes are obviously going to create wealth in the areas that will benefit and activate the local commercial banking systems, and as completion of the U.N. schemes are approached, more and more development financing will have to be undertaken by commercial banks. Once the food supplies are adequate, the housing up to U.N. standards, the water supplies adequate for the driest of seasons, the drainage and waste disposal working with no pollution of the environment and the education and health schemes in place and power supplies coming from renewable source then the role of the United Nations will be a maintenance one, rather than innovating development. This is when commercial development can take place if required, but it still must comply with the ultimate necessity of not polluting or ruining the local environment. Here the two banking systems must, and will, work closely together to control the increased cash flow that the new system will create. Recession and depressions in the world economy are always due to lack of adequate cash flow because the present financial system does not create this , for essential social and public services, when needed.

The two schemes or tiers of financing will take many years to achieve their objectives and when they have maintained the balanced environment that gives adequate employment to the local population, then it must continue to be financed by local effort, its financing being supplemented by the U.N. financial system, especially when natural disasters such as earthquakes, flooding, hurricanes and other catastrophes occur. The United Nations must maintain sufficient forces of military and civilian task groups which can be rushed into such disastrous areas as soon as they occur and they must be properly equipped, having the necessary backup transport and supplies. The scenes on the media of total incompetence to meet such situations is a prime example of the stupidity of Homo sapiens, and the failure of the world financial system to meet the needs of the species. The man-created disaster of the disease Aids spreading rapidly across the globe is an example of such incompetence to institute remedial action on a swift and global scale. Finance to meet this situation alone, if the species is to survive, should have been totally adequate and available yesterday.

6

Meeting Essential Needs On A World Scale

The first immediate problem that will have to be addressed by the United Nations when it introduces the new financial scheme on a world scale, is that it will raise the demand for essential foodstuffs. The increased amount of cash flowing to participating Nations will increase demand for such foodstuffs and further endanger the environment, unless a strict control is kept on production methods used to make the food available. Already in the last decade of the twentieth century there is less food in the world for more people, and if the world's fish, meat and grain were handed out equally, every person would have less to eat than five years previously.

In a Worldwatch Institute Report entitled "*Vital Signs in 1993: The trends that are shaping our future*" it reports that the population growth is outpacing available food. This is mainly because of record population growth, but also reflects that the main food suppliers, farms, ranches, and ocean fisheries, all appear to be approaching their maximum output (the Law of diminishing returns in operation). The report does contain some good news, child mortality is falling, people smoking less, bicycles are becoming more popular than cars, and wind power is growing faster than nuclear power, but it does show the major food systems are running into difficulties as attempts are made to expand supplies. The book length report says:

a: World grain production per person, although increasing one percent last year (1992) has fallen eight percent since reaching a high in 1984. There is a lack of growth in crop lands, water supplies and fertiliser use.

b: The world's oceans provided 97 million tons of fish for the third successive year, and some scientists believe they may never again yield the record 1989 peak harvest of 100 million tons. Seafood prices are rising around the world.

c: World meat production per person has started falling after four decades of general increase, with beef at its lowest in thirty years. Grasslands for grazing have been pushed to, or beyond the limits of their capacity on every continent.

Meanwhile, the population grew by 91 million in 1992 based on current growth rates, today's world population of 5.5 billion will double by 2030 (ie. in less than forty years if action is not taken, available food will be halved per head of the population and prices will be highly inflated.)

The report does note some more encouraging trends, in health, transport and energy, these are:

    a: The number of children in the world who die before their fifth birthday has fallen to 94 out of every 1,000 from 240 in the early fifties. The rate is still far higher in developing countries than in richer nations, 106 per 1,000 compared to 14.

    b: World wide cigarette production has dropped below 1,000 per person for the first time since 1984.

    c: More than 100 million bicycles were produced last year, continuing a trend that started in the Seventies. In the U.S.A. one in three people own a bicycle.

    d: In 1992 wind generators in California produced enough electricity to power San Francisco and Washington D.C.

The Worldwatch Institute Report shows the trend that is developing, because of the inadequate financial systems that cannot bring more land into useful cultivation and to halt the drying up of available land on the globe. The introduction of the new financial system, by raising the demand for food and other essential commodities, will cause initially even greater shortages and will make global planning even more essential than it is now. The United Nations will have to set up an Organisation to assess demand (much of this is already known but not based on the 2,500 calories per person per day globally), to organise production and distribution on a world-wide scale, and at the same time protect and enhance the environment on the earth's surface. This is a mammoth task, at present well beyond the scope and means of the world banking systems as they operate at the end of the twentieth century. But it is not beyond the scope of the proposed financial system that will make units of exchange available and will harness the mental and physical capacities of every human being according to their capabilities and not leave them to rot, mentally and physically, in the growing numbers of the unemployed that the present system is creating across the world.

Priorities of production will have to be laid down globally, and these must be basic cereals, fruits, and vegetables, before animal products, which take more land to produce food for humans. The global area devoted to pulse crops must also be increased as they not only produce vital protein for human sustenance, but also by being members of the Legume family of plants, increase the nitrogen in the soil by means of nitrogen fixing bacteria nodules on their roots which fertilise succeeding crops in the rotation. At the same time as the crop production is being increased, surveys must be carried out to find suitable areas of land that could quickly be brought into crop production by means of irrigation from desalination plants using electricity from wind generators, and extensive pipelines that convey the water to the crops in the new areas that need it, such as North Africa, southern Europe, the Middle East and many parts of Asia, Australia and South America. Many of these areas have produced valuable vegetation in the past, but become deserts because man has cut down their woodlands to produce fuel for warmth and cooking and timber for housing. Rain forest regions should be avoided as they are mainly suited to produce the fruits and nuts that grow in them naturally, and have soils and terrain unsuitable for changes in cropping. The present system of "setaside" in Europe and America must be reversed immediately in those areas known for their cropping capabilities as world surpluses will no longer exist and price stability and markets be assured under the exchange system.

Because the production of meat from land is less efficient in producing calories per acre, then meat production should be encouraged by feeding crop by-products, and by grazing those areas that because of soil type and climate are not suitable for cropping. In the northern hemisphere, steep hill land, mountainous regions and a return to mixed farming as practised in the early part of the twentieth century should be used to provide meat, while in the southern hemisphere the supply of water to desert lands should be used to produce herbage for stock to graze, and so start building up the fertility in those areas. Mixed farming of crops and stock, which has become unfashionable in many parts of the globe should be encouraged at all times to increase soil fertility and improve the condition of the soil's structure, as well as producing meat for the human diet.

The world-wide development of fish farming must be speeded up as a means of feeding the growing human population. This will mean the strict control of pollution of both rivers and tidal waters, so better sewage schemes and industrial waste disposal must also have high priority in financing food production. Fish is a meat that has a highly beneficial effect in the human diet and must be much more readily available than at present. As the Worldwatch report shows the production of the oceans is already decreasing while the human population is growing; the farming of fish in ponds, rivers and offshore fish pens must be encouraged and financed to double production in the next forty years or so.

Across the globe those engaged in plant breeding programmes should be encouraged to change from breeding varieties with high yields to those that give high calorie yields per hectare. At present many high yielding varieties are not necessarily high in calorific value, the increase in yield often being achieved by high moisture content. The varieties must also be sought that are best in local climates and soil conditions, thus giving the highest output possible per hectare. Regional, district and field climates must be accurately assessed and the variety grown must be suited to those particular conditions. Not enough attention is paid world-wide to doing this, and the output per hectare suffers accordingly. Here again a centralised information system will be needed to be drawn on by those advising the producers in each locality. The experience gained by the National Agricultural Advisory Services in Britain in the nineteen-fifties and after, in helping to increase national food production must be looked at and applied globally as soon as possible.

Alongside the centralised banking system should be an agricultural and environmental advisory system that will relate the production of an area to its climate, soil type and natural energy available. This will involve an effective education structure that gets across to all ages the right information on what they should be doing to achieve maximum output from their environment without destroying it for later generations. Time and effort should not be wasted on growing high cost but comparatively low yield crops, often involving high capital investment. Things like heated greenhouse cropping in low sunshine areas should obviously be discouraged or the planting of fruit orchards on heavy soils that require a lot of draining and remain cold later in the spring when growth should start early for maximum crop yield.

A great deal of attention should be paid to the natural topography of a region, together with its climate and availability of water, when making the choice of cropping to be recommended and used. Some high rainfall and damp areas should be used to produce timber crops that can be coppiced and its output used to produce fuel for timber burning electric generators for local household use, and possibly heat houses for the community. Such areas are often totally unsuitable for crops that require dry conditions for harvesting such as corn and hay, or for grazing animals who tread the ground into muddy conditions in the wet season and so lower output of calories per hectare. Many of the mountain valleys across Europe and America come into this category. With their ample supplies of wind and water they should be able to produce by hydroelectric schemes, wind farms and coppiced timber, electricity for sale to much less fortunate areas, in exchange for food, fodder and other daily essentials, instead of trying to produce crops from unsuitable land and climate.

The extension of large areas across the globe under crop production, besides needing adequate water, power and fertiliser supply and an adequate education system, will need an efficient transport infrastructure, either road or railway whichever is the most economical. Success in increasing output will depend on a reliable means of getting supplies into these areas, and crops and produce out to the nearest market or port. In areas of periodic high rainfall such as monsoons or rainy seasons, roads that can be washed away are often less successful than light or heavy railway tracks. Light railways in such areas have a proven record in the tropics on plantations of various types, and if built and drained properly will resist tropical monsoons far better than roads, which sometimes take weeks to repair or re-establish after the rainy season. Many of the Humanitarian Agencies trying to get bulk supplies into such areas in Africa, the Indian subcontinent and South America would have been more successful if such railway systems, criss-crossing the region, were already in place. Unfortunately they are not and road transport is held up for weeks or months on end with dire consequences for a starving population waiting for their aid.

Depending on the area and the right type of vehicle, storage facilities must be set up. Transport vehicles and carriages must be air conditioned, refrigerated or even heated to move perishable produce out of the production regions to the centres of high population and demand. This type of transport has been extensively developed in the Western World and food distribution presents little or no complications whatever the conditions, but in the Eastern block region when it was under communism this problem was neglected and the waste of produce in transport was horrendous creating the shortages that helped bring on the breakdown of the system. It was reported that potatoes from the production areas were transported in unheated trucks and arrived at the markets frosted and unusable in the hardest winter periods. Silos and grain stores were vermin and pest infected and not properly cleaned from one season to another, so crops in them were lost in storage. The Western "Know-how" in these matters must be harnessed and used across the globe to prevent the loss in calories for the growing world population.

With world-wide production being planned and co-ordinated for the most efficient use of the environment then many staple foods such as grains, fruit and meat will need to be moved from one part of the globe to areas where demand exceeds local supply. This will require a world merchant fleet of ships far greater than exists now.

Thus ship building will have to take place on a large scale, and this expansion of the mercantile fleet will need to be centrally directed as the building of the wrong type of vessel will be wasteful of time and resources. For example, as renewable energy supplies develop the need for oil tankers will decrease. Bulk carriers, grain carriers and refrigerated vessels will be in much greater demand as produce is shipped around. Many countries in the third world lack adequate port facilities and this will need to be planned, developed or improved, again providing valuable work for unemployed local populations and increasing their earning powers. Air transport of perishable goods should diminish as it is costly in energy use and causes an increase in air pollution. The time could well come in the future when jet planes become obsolete because of their high energy costs, then perhaps life will move at a slower, healthier pace than during the twentieth century.

To cut down on pollution of the atmosphere the most energy saving, low pollution means of powering transport from areas of production to areas of need must be developed and enforced. There is a need to look at moderate sized sea vessels using computer controlled sails and wind power to move non-perishable goods around the globe. Such vessels of moderate size would not only create employment but also be able to enter smaller ports than the vast bulk carrying vessels that have become the mainstay of the merchant fleets recently. Once unloaded at ports, then the removal of goods inland to the centres of need can be by efficient railways and canals rather than high speed motorway transport and land consuming road systems. The canals from ports could have two functions, one to carry desalinated water inland for use in irrigation systems, going up through banks of locks to higher ground and also to carry barge traffic bearing bulk goods such as grain, potatoes and other crops. If the canals are made wide enough and the barges big enough then other bulk imports, such as tractors, machinery, timber and building material, generating equipment etc. can also be transported. The establishment of such transport infrastructures across the globe in participating countries in the new financial scheme could take half a century to establish and provide ample employment while being set up, then run and maintained afterwards.

If the Worldwatch prediction of the population doubling in the next forty years is correct and comes about, all this increase in food production and the infrastructure to move it around, as well as feeding adequately the two thirds of the world population already underfed, needs to be started now or yesterday would be better. Civil and ethnic wars, as seen in the world already, will go on increasing merely to obtain enough food supplies for their own population groups. Those, with the armaments, will continue to seize available supplies and the unarmed and the weak will become poorer and starve under the present system. To stop this there must be central control by the United Nations Organisation to produce the necessary food, transport it safely to where it is needed and ensure it is fairly distributed to all who are in need, irrespective of their colour, creed and financial position. This is all too clearly not happening in the regions where the U.N. is trying to do it at the moment, ie. Somalia, Bosnia and Angola to mention but a few of the world's trouble spots that need calming and assistance. To achieve it effectively an International police force, made up of well armed and trained Units of ground, air and sea forces must be set up by the United Nations, not provided by individual Nations as at present, under the direct control of the General Assembly of the U.N. These could be a career force, serving the global population and not restricted by individual Governments. They must be prepared to fight the supplies through to starving people, or to disaster and famine areas, irrespective of what local governments may say, ie. such people as the Kurds and Marsh Arabs of Iraq should receive supplies.

The United Nations' experience in providing humanitarian aid, probably soon in South Africa, shows that the protection of food supplies must have a high priority in any International and national thinking as scarcity of food increases, and population numbers grow globally, then the criminal elements will move against basic necessities as they have into the drug markets across the world. Times of great shortage, be it money, work, food or other everyday necessities always increase corruption, exorbitant charging, prostitution and the general degrading of the population of an area suffering from the shortage. It is already seen on the media across the world in both western and third world nations. Even when humanitarian aid reaches an area always there are those who exploit the shortages of their own people to their own ends, be it money, sex or political power that is sought. Many in the Western Forces after World War Two saw it happening in those times of shortage, and it is recurring again in the ex-communist countries. It must be the function of a well financed United Nations operation to stop it as the population pressure creates more food shortages.

One of the main ways to check and eliminate such corrupt actions, is to ensure that all regions and countries across the world produce as much food as possible from their own resources. Available finance to provide water, housing and power supplies from renewable sources is essential to carry such a programme out. At the same time the local environment must be maintained and enhanced to counteract pollution and so ensure the production of food can be continued indefinitely. In many cases this will require a concentrated educational programme to train the labour and management to carry out such food production schemes and so provide money making employment within the community. The new finance by the SAP scheme is designed to do this, giving such work priority over all other financing, but as already has been stated it must be controlled by regions, using incorruptible staff, preferably not from the local region who are trained to assess the work priorities to increase and maintain food production in the area, and environmental improvements to enhance living and working conditions.

The regional banks set up under the SAP scheme must monitor and supervise food distribution in areas of acute shortage across the world population, be it the slum of British or American cities or those of India, China, South America or Africa. These Regional Banks must ensure adequate sums of financial units are available to the population to provide their basic needs of food, water, power, housing, waste disposal, and health facilities, but not to be squandered on luxury developments while the main population starves. The high office blocks of the Western World and the grand palaces of the ex-Communist world must be avoided or put to use to improve the living standards of the main populations without wasting finance on fresh ones. All power corrupts, but most of all does monetary power unless rigorously supervised and accountable to the people through the ballot box.

The stark fact that population growth and now shortage of time are beyond human control to a major degree, means that food production and its distribution must have the highest priority of the United Nations members. Coupled with this must be the production of essential industrial goods to meet the needs of food production, tools and machinery, low cost transport etc. It is no longer something that can be left to individual nations or the whim of political parties and their leaders. The environment in which it is all happening is finite and rapidly disappearing. Unfortunately sexual reproduction, like urination and defaecation are natural functions of a healthy (or unhealthy) human body and all are increasingly polluting and destroying the environment the species Homo sapiens requires to survive and live in. Unpopular as it may be to the individual, state or ethnic group, enforced central control, unbiased by religion and creed, must be practised at all levels of human society in future to ensure the continuation of the species. The United Nations with its global membership is the only source of control left to the human species.

This means that in-depth studies on how to achieve this control, must be established and carried on, at the same time as setting up the financial schemes related to population using the SAP unit of finance. The U.N.O., through its various agencies already has available a great deal of the facts needed, and other outside organisations like the Worldwatch Institute, University Research Departments, The International Monetary Fund, and various Government Statistics departments etc., must all be called upon to cooperate and make their information and statistics available to the study groups. The result of these studies must be drawn together and collated by the central planning department of the U.N. to use in forming and putting into operation the world plan of expanded food production.

At the same time as all this is being done a massive world wide programme of education and media co-operation must be set up to inform the world population of the impending dangers from their own individual actions. The global effect of those actions, and the part they each could play in curtailing and reversing them, must be impressed on them. Religion and social groups have an especial part to play in this education programme, and many of the teachings of religious groups may need to be reversed, especially in relation to birth control and size of family and their subsequent effect on the global environment. The mass media output that at present seems to revolve round sex and violence should begin to direct their message towards the effect of these actions on the local and world community and its environment, Somalia, Bosnia, Rwanda and Ireland would be good places to start to spread the message. The young in the world who today are particularly influenced by the information spread by the media should be targeted, to make them see the error of human ways from an early age, particularly to give them an in-depth understanding of the functions of their own bodies and the effect their own actions have on those functions, such as abuse by alcohol, drugs and smoking. In view of the time scale the species now lives under, all this should have been done yesterday, as the teenagers of today will have to carry out and put into action world-wide plans to curtail the population explosion.

7

A Community Structure For Self Preservation

Countries having the right democratic structure and electoral system to qualify for the SAP scheme of finance run by the United Nations Organisation, where their financial credit is based on their population numbers and their infrastructure needs, will have enough credit to set up local and national communities that can be self preserving. This means they will be capable eventually of providing their own requirements of food, housing, power supplies, waste disposal, health service and a proper education service. They should not be dependent on trade with too many outside areas to sustain their communities, as they will be working towards self sufficiency. It will be in the commercial section of the financial structure where trade will be carried on, and luxury goods they produce will be sold, or those they need will be purchased if they have the credit to do so.

With a rapidly growing population in many areas, to maintain the continuation of the human species in that area, the local environment, capable of sustaining that population, must be built up, and then preserved. This will mean an ordered and controlled community structure, very carefully planned, that has the environment central to its thinking, not its financial exploitation as happens under the existing means of wealth creation. This is the fundamental change of direction that the new scheme is capable of bringing about in the way that the species lives. Global preservation is central to the concept, and renewable energy supplies and recycling are essential to this.

If the species Homo sapiens is to survive then they are going to have to accept that they are all part of the global community and forego their own social, religious or political hobby horses which at present they follow. As John Donne wrote four centuries ago, "No man is an Island ..... every man ..... is part of the main", otherwise the bell will "toll for thee" Homo sapiens! To do this will require a community structure that is disciplined and controlled, hence the insistence on people or proportional representation, at all levels of society to take part in the new financial scheme. If all voters do not have the right to have their views heard and take part in the Country's government and in regional and local councils, then secular, political or economic pressure groups will dominate and the structure to maintain an ecology fit for man to continue to exist in will not survive the treatment it is at present receiving. All political systems that at present allows one party to dominate the government must be changed to stop one such party dominance and allow the community to become part of the global scheme of survival. Countries such as America, Britain, Russia, Iran, Iraq, South Africa and many others at this present time will need to make changes in their electoral and government methods.

People or proportional representation will enable the truly democratic process to be in charge of the community structure, because voters will have voted for a representative nearest to their own views on the committee, council or government. They should not feel detached from the governing process as they so often do with present systems. The leaders or organisers of these various committees will be appointed for their experience and personality and because the majority of voters have faith that they will work for the good of the whole community and not their own political party or view. Any form of political dogma must be ignored and excluded from the voting process. The building up and maintenance of the ecology for both now and future generations must be the policy to be followed so the local, and eventually the global, environment is improved and enhanced. Party politics are outdated and irrelevant in this situation, as they cannot claim to make the environment and the preservation of the species the first priority instead of the party's dogma. Survival time for the species is now too short to continue following political beliefs. As President Gorbachov said back in 1985 "We cannot go on living like this."

Because the new financial system will provide basic finance for the essentials of the social structure, as a right based on population numbers, the only cost being the administrative ones, then taxation to raise this basic finance will be unnecessary. This will immediately raise the spending power of the individual and enable them to keep a higher proportion of their earnings for the use of themselves, or their families. Taxation must be used to control excessive misuse of the local environment and too much profit taking in the commercial and industrial sections of the two tier finance system, especially when the money making comes from environmental sources and means the local resources are being exploited for private profit. In the European economy water and gas supplies immediately come to mind where excessive profits are made out of the local resources. Another area for high taxation would be where prime mineral reserves of the earth's surface are being used and huge profits taken; or possible recycled materials are being ignored. Exploitation of glass, metals, paper and timber resources without recycling are possible sources of taxation that spring to mind in such circumstances. Another situation that must be taxed is where excessive pollution of the air, local water supplies or by noise, takes place to the annoyance of the local community. In all cases the taxation should be crippling enough to deter or stop the exploiters from carrying on their operations, or force them to change their methods to more environmentally friendly methods.

Under the new financial order the majority of any community should be employed or engaged in improving and preserving their local and the area environment. This is a much higher proportion than is possible under the present system of financing public works, and will reduce the necessity to have industrial and commercial work places for the majority of a local population. In reducing the importance of so called wealth producing activities, and replacing them with basic infrastructure employment, individuals will feel they have an important part to play in the community structure. Under the present system many people are made to feel irrelevant to the main social activities within the community. The work to be done in maintaining the local infrastructure will stretch right across the whole spectrum of employment from producing food and distributing it, housing and its maintenance, drainage and waste disposal;, recycling of all reusable materials, local transport of people and goods, health and hospitals, care for all sections of the community including the very elderly, to the expanded education structure that will be needed. The future generations must be taught to see that they have an essential part to play in the community structure, and be trained to take part in it, not to feel unwanted from the time they leave school as the present system makes them, because there is no meaningful employment for them in the community.

The building up of this new environmental preserving and community structure will mean a massive education programme will be needed from the onset of a country entering the scheme. This will have to be undertaken at all levels of society, from the top management responsible for introducing the scheme, right through all age groups to the latest recruit leaving school with the minimal academic qualification, no one must feel left out and unwanted in the community. A growing section of the population feel unwanted and out of the main stream of society and this makes them turn to crime against the majority, whom they see as being more fortunate than themselves. This is especially true amongst unemployed school leavers who need motivation to become part of the adult community. The education of individuals at all strata in society will need constant updating so they know the changing situation within the community and how to deal with it. The media has a responsible part to play in this. The young still within the full time education section of their lives, the young marrieds rearing their children, and the retired, all have an essential part to play in preserving their local environment and must be educated and updated in their knowledge to do this. Those in industry and commercial work forces must also have constant access to further education and may transfer to use their special skills in the environment maintenance process.

The growing rapidity of the breakdown of the ability of the earth's environment to maintain the massive growth in the human population must concentrate human thinking on the way society is living. Homo sapiens must accept much more control in the way they live and control of the community structure is central to this, this control starts from the smallest units. In rural areas individual farms and holdings will have a responsibility to their local parishes which are part of small districts that will make up the region.

These regions will all be part of a national structure whose community function will be to co-ordinate the preservation control of their environment, and supervise the funding request to the United Nation's funds. Most continents will have a number of national structures in them and to a certain extent the U.N. will have to see that the plans across a continent do not work in opposition to each other. Where the continents are vast, as in the case of the Americas, Africa, Asia and Europe, then changes in climate types will require different types of control enforcing.

Control of communities in urban areas, because of the smaller land areas involved than the rural situation, will mean that climatic influences will not be so varied. Here control must again start with the units of individual works, factories and their residential communities around them. These again could be responsible to the local parishes, then to small districts and then to the town or city depending on the population involved. These towns or cities must co-operate with their surrounding rural districts and regions to preserve the environment they all live in, and make it as self supporting as it can be. In highly populated areas such as Europe, parts of the Middle East and elsewhere the co-operation between rural and urban areas to sustain their local ecology must be very close and the communities work very much together in their planning. Destruction of rural areas by cities, which has already taken place across the globe, must be stopped in the cause of ecological preservation.

The pressing time factor now makes it essential to all this control that the environment is preserved and enhanced. Pollution must be eliminated, work must be provided for all members of the community as well as the disabled and the less able members of society. The maintenance of the social structure of housing, power supplies, water and drainage, waste disposal, health facilities and the education structure, are fundamental rights of all human beings and should not be denied through lack of funding or non-democratic government. It is well within the grasp and ability of human society that no one, born on to this earth, should be in need of the basic essentials of life, providing they conform to the social and community structure that will be set up, and if they work to maintain and improve that structure. It is their basic humanitarian right under the United Nations Charter set up all those years ago, but not yet achieved because of the stupidity of the present financial and political systems.

Central to the success of maintaining and enhancing the local environment is the use of renewable energy resources and the recycling of waste and all other materials. Fossil fuels are finite resources on this globe and already the end of their availability is in sight. Because of pollution and the cost of extraction, coal is being run down and cannot be used much longer. Gas supplies are just as indefinite and may not last long into the next century, making the electricity policy of the present British Government an extremely foolish and short-sighted one. Oil reserves also are strictly limited, many already think that they should not be wasted on fuelling transport but reserved for the chemical industry so as to prolong their availability. Nuclear fuels are far too expensive to produce and the radiation problems that occur during their use, and the disposal of their waste, are far too hazardous to life on the globe for their use to be continued as a source of power. The human species may yet disappear overnight like the dinosaurs because of a gigantic nuclear accident somewhere in the world by some careless operator, as happened at Chenobyl in Russia. The recycling of waste and other materials must not pollute, but must be operated to the maximum so making the necessity to use prime materials from the globe surface kept to a minimum, especially oxygen in the atmosphere and clean water across the globe. Materials that can be grown such as timber, oil rape seed etc. should be concentrated upon while it should be an offence to waste metal that can be recycled and so not dug up from the earth's surface as basic ore.

The production of renewable energy starts in every sewage works across the world, in the interest of cutting pollution of water supplies, every group of houses should be served by a sewage cleansing plant with a digester process that produces methane gas to be used to generate electricity, and digested sewage sludge to be returned to the land locally to build up soil fertility. Such sewage cleansing plants could be produced as packages in sizes to suit the number of houses to be served and readily available, the gas generators could come with the package. Farms with large livestock units, be they cattle, pigs, horses or poultry could also be cleansed by such sewage cleansing plants, again helping to cut down slurry pollution by producing a digested compost from the slurry waste of the livestock unit. The manufacture of such sewage cleansing plants should be researched and their output for the market will need a high priority. SAP finance would of course automatically be available for such schemes across the globe, as a priority to cut down on land and water pollution.

For coastal areas across the globe, the new concept of tidal stream turbines driving electric generators must be researched, developed, manufactured and installed round coast lines of the world where suitable tidal flows occur. While this concept is at an early stage of development it has tremendous potential for harnessing the energy generated by the moon's influence on water masses of the globe. By this means the tidal currents of any significance could be captured to produce power for man's use. They would be like Windfarms under the sea, but not making so much noise or be visually intrusive, as some objectors find wind farms. Recent reports estimate that twenty per cent of the U.K.'s power supply could come from this means, and at considerably less cost than nuclear or gas fired generators. The turbines are anchored to the seabed in areas of strong currents and held up by a buoy on the surface to swing in the tidal currents. Eventually it might be possible to develop rafts on the surface holding up the tidal turbines beneath and having wind generators above in the air, so doubling the electricity output from each installation. In this case much more than 20% of the U.K.'s power requirements might well be generated. Again SAP finance would automatically be available to set such installations up as they increase the global energy production, and the calories available for communities to use.

There is nothing new in the use of wind or air movements to provide energy for man's needs. Since mediaeval times windmills have been used to grind grain and later to pump water. During the period of the industrial revolution they were neglected because fossil fuels, coal and later oil provided a more reliable source of energy, especially for transport, although sailing ships are still in common use for sea transport. As the end of cheap fossil fuels approaches, man has been turning to wind power once again, and wind powered generators grouped in farms have sprung up across the globe and will continue to do so as the demand for such units reduces the purchase price and makes them more readily available for less fortunate countries. Winds across the world are increasing in strength, especially with the cutting down of vast areas of forests which used to absorb the movement of air in their foliage and so diminish the force that wind generated. In desert areas, like the oceans, there is nearly always air movement that could be used to generate electric power; equipment to do this is comparatively easy to install and maintain. High priority of financing should again be given to set up and operate this form of renewable energy, so utilising a very cheap and readily available source. Some people do object to the noise these generators make but in time manufacturers will cut down on the noise and where power did not previously exist, noise is a small price to pay for the availability of such a valuable asset to improving living standards.

Like windpower, water has been used as a means of producing energy since early times in human development, mills driven by large water wheels, even in comparatively flat areas have been in use for centuries in the Western world and in China. These water wheels were fed by leats bringing water down from higher up the local river or stream. Many still exist and operate in both rural areas and in small towns. They are a valuable way of distributing water about the countryside. Here again generators could be powered by such water supplies and supplement local needs, but it is in hilly and mountainous regions that hydropower is extremely efficient at providing energy from turbo-driven generators. The ultimate in use of water power is where the water is recycled and used again and many such schemes already exist. There is one in north Wales where the mountain reservoir drives the turbine generator all day, the water is held after driving the generators and when demand for electricity drops then the electricity generated drives pumps to carry the water stores back up the mountain to fill the top reservoir and so be used again.

Here man has almost achieved the Alchemist's search for perpetual motion – but some water loss does occur. With hydro power like other sources of natural energy, time, and the production of the necessary plant must be given to achieve results.

Space technology has enabled man to harness the power of the sun's rays both to produce electricity to work machines and charge batteries. It can also be used through solar panels on the roofs of houses to heat water for domestic use and for central heating. In colder climates solar heated houses have already been built and found to be very effective. The use of this power in high sunshine areas has a great future if the technology is developed properly, especially in Third World countries where cooking by wood has been traditional since early times in civilisation. This has always entailed cutting down the adjacent forests to the settlements and the denuding of the soils, starting the process of desert formation. Electricity produced from solar panels could generate heat for cooking and water heating and so do away with the necessity to use wood. Once the technology has been developed with SAP financing and mass production reduced the cost of manufacture, then the cost of installing such systems world-wide in high sunshine areas will be a very big step towards saving the environment in those areas. Solar heated houses could become the norm in all suitable places so reducing the need to provide other forms of energy. The use of wood for heating and cooking could eventually be almost eliminated, all waste wood products at present so used then made available to convert into wood chips and building materials as part of the recycling campaign and so build up the tree population across the globe.

As mentioned in the last chapter, in high rainfall areas and at latitudes where food crops cannot be successfully grown, then tree crops for coppicing and burning in furnaces can generate electricity. This again would provide purposeful work in areas that are not suitable for much else and the electricity produced could be used by the local community, the surplus fed into the national electricity of the respective country where it was being carried out. As in other new means of energy production this will require the manufacture of suitable plant, to be used in the locations where tree crops, such as willow, chestnut etc., that respond to coppicing treatment can be grown. Substantial areas of trees will have to be planted to provide enough output to keep the furnaces fed and the generators working. But it will produce renewable energy without using up the earth's resources, and provide meaningful work for populations in areas where unemployment is always high; most important of all it will create vast areas of trees and their leaves that will convert excess water into oxygen producing trees to refurbish the supply in the atmosphere, and so help to replace the vital element that mankind is using too rapidly.

Central to preserving and enhancing the ecology of the globe for Homo sapiens to continue living on it, is the recycling of everything that it is possible to recycle. This must be the aim of all community living, so that nothing is wasted at any time. By doing this the use of fossil fuels can rapidly be diminished and eventually, when the system is working effectively across the globe, the need for such fuels to be used, totally eliminated. Many recycling systems have long been in use such as the re-melting of scrap iron and aluminium by mixing these with new metals produced from ore, reducing the extraction of ore from the crust of the earth. More recently the world population has been encouraged to recycle paper and glass and this should be made compulsory as a continual operation. In all recycling schemes a certain amount of waste will occur but the new material produced will greatly diminish the need to cut timber for paper or dig silica for glass production. Another less obvious form of recycling is to encourage manufacturers to produce goods with reusable parts, or ensure they are easily melted down after use. The automobile industry has already started along this path of production and could expand the practice right across the range. In future tax incentives should be offered to encourage them along this route to preserve the globe's resources. They produce one of the greatest users of the earth's oxygen and will do so until they stop using internal combustion engines as a source of power for their vehicles. Manufacturers of plastic goods should only use those types of plastic that can be recycled and all plastic should be biodegradable by law in future.

One of the major causes of pollution on the globe at present is the dumping of waste, from nuclear by-products causing radiation hazards to simple domestic and industrial waste dumped in landfill sites which pollute the local sources of water across a large area. To cut down and eliminate this must be the main aim of the world recycling programme. Waste of an organic nature should always be shredded and composted by bacterial action and returned to the topsoil of the earth to enhance and build up the organic content so helping to convert mineral predominant topsoils into rich loam, thus having a higher crop bearing potential. As these operations are labour intensive it would provide meaningful work for a section of the community, enhance the cropping potential of the local soils and distribute waste, including sewage waste, in a way that improves the local environs. This again should have a high priority in funding under the new SAP scheme. Chemical and industrial wastes may be more difficult to deal with, but again finance must be made available to eliminate them in the pursuit of global preservation and the enhancement of the ecology for mankind.

All the activities already mentioned both to preserve and improve a community's environment should be funded from the United Nations under the SAP scheme, according to the population of an area. Under the U.N. Charter these are basic human rights and should not be denied to any member of the human species on financial grounds. The SAP scheme funding using energy units of a fixed value is a right to every person on the globe who accepts the simple rules laid down for membership of the scheme. The work involved in a community of maintaining and enhancing the local environment, to provide the right ecology for the human species to continue to exist indefinitely in that area of the globe, will occupy a major section of that community and so provide employment for those who today are unemployed through lack of capital and revenue expenditure on maintaining the ecology. The remuneration for such work will be funded so that a living wage, housing at affordable prices, plus efficient basic services, health care and access to a meaningful education, are available to all who live in the area. No person, government or committee should have the right to deny this to an individual, providing they accept the rules of society and the rights of their fellow beings. The preservation and improvement of the environment is a paramount need if Homo sapiens is to survive.

One area of pollution of the earth's surface that every community living on ancient sites of civilisation is going to have to tackle is the previous pollution by old industries and life styles that did not understand the damage they were doing to the local ecology. This is especially so in many areas of Eastern Block countries where industrial pollution was allowed to ruin whole sections of the countryside and is still continuing because funds do not exist to clean up the area. Nuclear pollution by the Chenobyl disaster is one such case and the continuing arguments about the Sellafield site in Northern Britain shows how man's activities have imposed a dangerous situation on the safety of whole areas for Homo sapiens to live in. Many buildings, old factory sites, tips, agricultural land and mining sites are worn out, polluted to a dangerous level, often by lead, arsenic and other highly dangerous chemicals used in, or dumped during previous industrial activities and production methods. In the British Isles alone it has been estimated by Industrial Organisations that it will cost billions of pounds to bring them up to modern standards so they can be used again.

A parallel problem that communities have to address is the old housing, built either in the period of rapid industrial expansion or before, found in many British, European, Asian etc. towns and cities that in no way meet modern standards of housing for the area's climate. They are overcrowded, lack proper ventilation, are damp, and the drainage is in many cases primitive or non existent. Besides being a health hazard to those expected to live in them, they contribute greatly to the pollution and destruction of the area. Many high rise housing estates built to a limited budget across the world since World War Two, come into this category and will also need pulling down and replacing with accommodation that complies with modern building standards for the region and climate. Under the present economic system funds are not available to do this even in the so called wealthy Western countries, let alone to build new housing of such standards in the developing Third World. This problem alone could occupy all communities for the next century or longer. All households are entitled to environmentally modern homes, that conserve energy, guarantee healthy living standards and cut pollution of their local environment.

Much of the community structure that has been talked about in this chapter is already in place across many countries of the world, especially in those regions or continents that have been colonised in the past. A controlled community structure was one of the good things that colonisation imposed on communities, just to make them function reasonably efficiently. With the United Nations finance scheme imposing a fair democratic structure on all countries participating, everyone aged eighteen or over will not only have a vote that counts, but also will feel they are part of the community, helping to maintain their local environment and enhancing the community life style by the work they do. All this will provide employment for all physically and mentally capable of taking part, with the young, the disabled and the old being cared for in the community. It will, of course, take a long time to achieve, especially in the more backward problem areas where ethnic, religious or secular interests exist, such as the former Eastern Block States, Asia or even parts of modern Europe like Bosnia and Serbia. It cannot happen under the present financial system where profits have to be produced at the environment's expense, to pay for progress, and many undemocratic countries and states will not want it to happen and so ruin their present lifestyle and power structure. But, for the sake of the environmental preservation and enhancement so that the species Homo sapiens can continue to exist, International pressure must be bought to bear on such states to make them conform and contribute to global preservation.

8

The New Commercialism And Industrialism

Under the new two tier system of finance to improve the ecology and save Homo sapiens, the second tier that finances Commerce and Industry must also cut back on its demand on global resources, especially water, and oxygen in the atmosphere. Excess production of unwanted goods must be avoided so as to economise in the use of energy. Modern production methods across the world have become too dependent on excessive use of energy in the interest of speeding production to increase output and the profit margin. This is particularly so in the United States that still uses more than 40% of the world's energy consumption and most of that could be said to be unnecessary. The Japanese, with their growing Industrialisation across the globe will soon overtake the U.S.A. and once China becomes a major Industrial power, the world's energy reserves, except for the renewable ones, will soon be exhausted.

For the next half century or longer commercial, and industrial production will have to be concentrated on supplying the vastly increased demand, generated by the new first tier finance system for enhancing the environment. Supplies of equipment and capital goods will be needed for the vastly expanded services across the globe; these will include, irrigation and water pumping supplies, Agricultural machinery, wind and water generators, sewage and digester equipment, shipping and transport equipment from railway lines to heavy earth moving trucks, essential housing equipment and materials including blocks, tiles, piping, electrical goods and insulation materials. The demand will be tremendous once the financial "log jam" is removed from world trading, and energy use and the destruction of the earth's resources must be kept to a minimum so much research and development must go into those two problems.

To finance all this the world's Commercial Banking organisation must work closely with the United Nation finance Bank structure to control where commercial and industrial finance is invested, so that unnecessary waste of resources are avoided. The new capital resources, based on population numbers can only be directed into feeding the population adequately and into environment enhancement projects, and the Banks will have to observe this aim until the world ecology is improving. This aim will have to continue for a very long time until the world's water supplies become pure and unpolluted, and the oxygen content of the atmosphere and ozone layer above it, is increasing at an annual rate that will eventually achieve its predetermined level of the Middle ages.

Finance of infrastructure work must, for a very long time take priority over purely commercial and industrial consideration. This may mean the direction of resources into meeting the infrastructure needs, so that demands by communities or regions for adequate housing, schools, hospitals and clinics, transport amenities and all the other backup services already listed, must be completed and sufficient for local communities before non essentials such as offices, industrial estates, leisure and sports facilities etc., are built or provided. The stupidity of investment as occurred in the eighties (in Britain) when unwanted office blocks were built, to stand empty, while the homeless slept in their doorways at night, and public services such as hospitals, schools, road repairs etc., were starved of investment, must not be repeated across the globe.

Many industries are notorious for their ability to destroy the environment, either through their methods of production or the way their products use up valuable resources, especially oxygen. The armaments industry world-wide is one of the worst in this respect, then the motor industry that depends on the internal combustion engine for their power, and the nuclear industry whose by-products are impossible to dispose of and from which a chance accident could be world destroying. All these and many others that encourage the use of fossil fuels should be restricted, drastically curtailed or stopped until they start producing environment enhancing methods of production and their products improve and do not destroy the global ecology. The best method of restricting them is to subject them to crippling taxation that forces them to change their ways or go out of production. The present stupid system of subsidising nuclear energy production must be stopped and used for alternative energy systems instead. As nuclear energy is not competitive with existing systems of energy production, let alone renewable ones, it would soon go out of use and become part of the energy history.

From the onset of the new financial scheme it is essential to cut demand for non essential products that the mass of the world population can do without. A long list of such non essentials can be drawn up, from over-luxurious housing and offices using an unnecessary amount of hardwood timbers, expensive stonework such as marble and alabaster, to grandiose leisure facilities using heat, light and water which few people can afford or have the time and energy to use, and are consequently non-paying and heavily subsidised; in proportion to the overall provision of sports facilities such as playing fields, cycle tracks etc., that the mass of the population can use, especially when at school. An example of the environment wasting extravagant provisions are the four yearly Olympic Games which have to be made by the host country! Another overprovision of non essential goods are the vast amount of small goods and "Knick-Knacks" now produced and advertised on T.V. and by mail order firms involving vast amounts of materials and energy that the world cannot spare. All this overprovision should be heavily taxed off the market in the interest of conservation of the earth's resources.

The "service" industries, particularly since computerisation, now use excessive amounts of electrical energy that will not be available when fossil fuels run out. Nor can the world afford the excess profits of so called "risk" insurance, where individuals obtain excessive returns from high premiums for insurance which most of the insured cannot afford. The Chief Executive in Britain who recently was paid a bonus of twenty six million pounds on car insurance takings is an obvious misuse of the world's financial resources. Such high profits must be taxed and returned for the benefit of the ordinary consumer, until such individuals are receiving payments and incomes in line with average earnings across the globe. Such excessive incomes must be penalised by tax and "ploughed back" into the enhancement of the ecology for Homo sapiens to survive as a species.

Under the new financial scheme, costing will be based on energy units, the SAP unit, and this will ensure that energy use will be cut in the interest of lowering costs. Into such costings will be written fixed profit margins, and on non essential goods these margins will be limited by taxation, to return the excessive energy units made into the essential work of environment enhancement. The profit margin on any operation should never exceed 10% maximum, and above that figure any profit should be subject to 100% taxation to discourage exploitation of demand due to scarcity of that product. To enforce this will need detailed and careful inspection and control by the banking and taxation offices, because scarcity always leads to "black" or unauthorised markets developing and an expansion of illegal trading. This has happened since the introduction of V.A.T. at high rates leading to mushrooming of car boot sales across the British Isles. These now have an estimated turnover of over a billion pounds a year, none of which is subject to VAT, causing a taxation loss of millions of pounds to the national revenue. The human mind is adept at getting round taxation regulations.

One of the main causes of losses of financial resources is the high rate of interest charged on loans; this causes the borrower to have to exploit the earth's resources of even more profits to pay the interest charges. Many of the business failures and bankruptcies of the present recession come about because returns made on loans are insufficient to pay the interest charges. Under the new system, to avoid this happening, there will be a limit on interest paid on Monies borrowed, so returns on investments made by lenders will not be too high. This must especially apply to loans made under the existing credit card system where high interests are charged on them. Here again a ten percent maximum should be the limit that borrowers have to pay. Money lent for long term environment enhancement projects that do not come under the local or regional loan scheme should have a guarantee of not losing their capital, and a set return on that investment or borrowing at low interest rate of 3-5% until repaid. This will encourage individuals to borrow to enhance their local environs.

Such a guarantee would mean that commercial Banks would be obliged to give loans to individuals or groups in a community who wish to carry out environmental enhancement that is not part of the local or regional scheme. In the event of the failure by the individual to repay the loan or the interest, then the bank should be able to claim compensation from the U.N. central funds and so be able to write off the loss involved. Such a system is lacking in the present time and would encourage individuals to borrow money not only to improve their own environs but to remove some of the existing eyesores that are not commercially attractive to tackle and improve. Such things as derelict buildings, badly sited buildings, waste areas such as old quarries and industrial dumps, come into this category, not tackled now because of lack of funds or lenders to make such capital available.

Some industries are very destructive of the environment and in many cases pollute the area around them to such an extent that it will be hundreds of years before they have re-established themselves in a natural way. The armament and chemical Industries have been notorious for this and many areas in Britain and elsewhere that were centres for them will be derelict for a very long time. To avoid this happening in future such production as is necessary will have to be regulated world-wide, so that all operate within the controls laid down by the United Nations. The type of armaments and chemicals produced must be strictly under the U.N. so as to control the damage to the environment, and to the population who have to live and work in that area around such licensed production centres. Too many regions of the world have already been devastated to allow such destruction to continue. The continual switch from fossil fuels and the closing down of mining operations, either deep pit or opencast, will help to slow and eventually stop, such devastation, although closed pits will continue to pour polluted water out into the surrounding countryside unless properly managed after closure. This is already happening in Britain and across the globe and clean up will take many, many years and a lot of expense.

Once the majority of nations have joined the United Nations' financial scheme and the majority of world trade is based on fixed value energy units, this will open up and increase production of basic supplies of essential goods. These must include foods, clothing, domestic equipment for households, toilet and sanitary requirements, simple medicines especially antiseptics and contraceptives, and they all must be produced in such quantities as to be distributed world-wide and be equally available to all, as will be their entitlement under the new financial scheme. This will be a vast task for commerce and industry to tackle to supply the existing 5.5 Billion world population and the ever growing numbers of the people who will be produced in the next century if the estimated doubling of the population takes place.

To avoid rapid inflation and black market in trading developing because demand exceeds supply in the initial years of the scheme, it will be necessary and essential to maintain fixed pricing of goods based on the energy units, this will have to be enforced across the globe. The price of everyday essentials under the new scheme must not be forced up by shortages but strictly regulated. Industries must expand their output to meet increasing demand, and finance based on population growth will be able to do this, creating employment and avoiding the lowering of basic living standards. This is happening in the Western World at the moment due to the failure of the present system which is incapable of producing the capital for investment to produce such basic essentials. The political unrest in the Western World at this time is due to the financial system failing to meet basic demands of the growing population, and all political parties being unable to produce a workable solution to the problem, neither are they able to work with other political parties to correct the situation – hence the need for people or proportional representation to involve all sections of the community in the process of government. Under the new scheme investment will be directed by the commercial Banks to increase output where shortages are occurring, giving this priority over all other lending.

When demand exceeds supply, as is already happening in many of the Eastern Block countries, in parts of Europe and the Asian countries, where governments are unable to control and stop such exploitation; then criminal elements in society will try to exploit the shortages and control by terrorism. making big profits by doing so. This will be a major control problem for the United Nations, as they have already found in Bosnia and Somalia, and now Rwanda, only International co-operation by all communities will overcome this. A further initial danger will be that Governments not qualifying for the U.N. finance scheme, because of their political system, may themselves engage in such activities, especially those producing drugs etc. where they can produce in quantity due to their special climatic conditions. As in Serbia, frontier controls and sanctions by the rest of the world may be the only way of overcoming this and persuading such governments to join the new scheme and let their population benefit from the advantages, so also helping to enhance their environment and its contribution to improving the world environment.

To enable the United Nations to enforce and control the running of the new scheme it must have an International Police Force or Army, run and financed centrally, and not dependent on member state contributions, to carry out the enforcement of the International scheme. This must be an organisation recruited from all participating nations, the recruits being loyal to the U.N. force, and not their own nations, and of the highest standard of ability and professionalism so that people can trust this force to be unbiased and unbribable. Such a force (run by an International Organisation) has never existed before and will require a high standard of ability from its recruits and serving members. They must be equipped with armaments of the highest quality on land, air and sea. Operations and resistance may be met in any of the theatres in enforcing International law and order. The stupid situation that the United Nations is trying to cope with in various theatres across the globe must be settled by sanctions and a superior force if necessary. The earth can no longer afford civil wars and puppet warlords who want to exploit their own population. Basic humanitarian aid must be available to all, even if that country is not actively taking part in the U.N. scheme.

In the interest of future generations, enhancement and rapid improvement of the environment must be the first priority of all commercial and industrial operations, these must work to a list of priorities drawn up by the United Nations. Non essential and luxury goods will not feature on this list. Many of the environment destroying products - the internal combustion engine, power stations using fossil fuels to generate electricity, advertising by neon and other lights, too many television channels, must be phased out in the interest of saving energy and the earth's resources. To attract firms to supply this priority list, commercial banks should be required to offer low interest rates to those wishing to supply the essentials on the list, while firms wishing to produce non essentials must be charged a very high interest rate that will more than discourage them to attempt such production. The level of global destruction now reached is such that International laws on conservation must overrule financial considerations.

The destruction of the global environment, especially the loss of the ozone layer and oxygen in the atmosphere, and the pollution of the earth's waters, is so advanced that commercial and industrial production really needs placing on a controlled and directed basis internationally as was exercised in World War Two. This would entail goods being licensed as being environmentally essential before firms are permitted to produce them. This would cut down the waste of energy and of valuable materials in producing luxuries and unwanted goods. Such controls should continue to be enforced until the 5.5 billion of the world population (or whatever the then figure is) have been catered for with the basic essentials of life as already listed.

Under the supervision of the International Global Saving structure, run by the United Nations, communities and nations should be required to work closely together on environment enhancement. This would ensure that their local available labour and their local skills, produced by their education system should be directed into improvement, not destruction of their local ecology. This will almost certainly need finance and subsidy from the new central funds based on the population numbers and on the amount of previous destruction of the environment that has occurred. For example, to reclaim and re-vegitate desert areas along the North African coast would require heavy subsidisation for decades to come, and may even need a repopulation programme to carry out the work. The latter could be achieved by depopulation of the overcrowded cities and towns along that coast by offering them purposeful employment and better living standards in the countryside that is being reclaimed. It is envisaged that enhancement of the local environment to rebuild the local ecology will always involve the movement of population from local overcrowded towns and cities, back to the replanted and re-vegetated countryside, which has improved facilities to maintain a bigger population in more attractive conditions with subsidised living standards, until self sufficient.

The present much vaunted concepts of Free Trade Areas being discussed and built up by various continents, eg. Europe, the Americas and the Pacific Areas can only lead to further undirected destruction of these continents' environments in the interest of promoting trade and producing wealth under the existing financial system. Historically, free trading to produce wealth, world wide, has destroyed the ecology of Homo sapiens quicker than the previous two million years. Population growth always compounds this situation. One of the ancient Greek philosophers wrote "once man cuts down a wood to create a town, then a desert will be formed in that area." Homo sapiens now has sufficient knowledge and technology to reverse this situation, what is lacking is the finance to put it into action and the overall global direction to see that all communities improve their local environment. Industry and commerce must always work in with this concept.

The second tier of the new financial scheme should not fear control and direction by the United Nations in their efforts to save the world environment. Since the Industrial Revolution the demand for infrastructure development, towns, cities, railways, roads, airports and seaports, armaments on land, sea and air have all been the controlling factors in producing wealth by exploiting the earth's resources. The result has been the global destruction that is endangering the species. Now the globe must have a post-industrial era through sheer necessity to protect the species. Food production, the enhancement of the water and atmosphere, the switch to renewable energies and the total elimination of pollution of the habitat should be the control and direction of free enterprise, financed by energy units based on population numbers, not profit taking from global destruction, which has been the mainstay of the existing financial system. It will be a long and tedious path to follow, but it must be followed if this intelligent species is to survive indefinitely.

The Rebuilding Of The Global Environment

The survival of all species, whether Homo sapiens or any other species that evolved in the pre-industrial era of the world, is dependent on the clean air they breathe containing not less than 21% oxygen and little or no carbon dioxide or monoxide. The water they drink must be clean and pure, unpolluted by harmful chemicals or high levels of disease causing organisms such as salmonella, cholera, typhoid etc. Already in two thirds of the world over four fifths of all disease and one third of all deaths are caused by contaminated water. In a growing number of countries across the globe the amount of rainfall they receive is less than they need for their growing population numbers, some of their rivers are drying up and not reaching the seas as they used to. In Western America the water shortage is critical, none of the great Colorado river that carved out the spectacular Colorado Gorge now reaches the seas of the Pacific Ocean but has been used by man. In the great cities of the world, especially in the Western ones, respiratory diseases and deaths from them are increasing due to polluted, impure and oxygen short air, whose content has dropped well below 21% oxygen, mainly due to the excessive amounts of carbon dioxide and shortage of oxygen used up by the internal combustion engine's demand on the atmosphere.

Population growth and the excessive demands of industry on the air and water supplies are essential reasons for scrapping the present economic system that uses the destruction of the earth's resources to maintain itself, and attempts to produce wealth to meet the economic demands of the growing populations. It is vital to adopt, as soon as feasible, an economic scheme of trading that is based on energy units, readily available to population demands, at the same time enhancing and restoring the global environment. The first essential step in doing this is to restore the tree population across the globe to the level that existed on the land mass prior to the existence of Homo sapiens with its so called advanced "intelligence". Only when the tree population's production of oxygen exceeds the rate of use by the human population will the global atmosphere begin to return to the stage where it has surplus oxygen to replace the ozone layer across the world. At the same time all pollution of water supplies must be stopped by recycling through the earth all agricultural and domestic waste waters. All this work needs to start immediately and finance from the new scheme provided to do it without incurring crippling debts by those who do it. The human species must recognise the debt that they owe to those who undertake the clean up work, be it animal or vegetable.

Once the new finance scheme is accepted and established by the democratic countries of the world, then the long term plan to rebuild the global environment must proceed as quickly as possible. The plan should be divided into two main regional types, those with adequate rainfall and river waters, and those without adequate rainfall where deserts are already well established or are becoming established in the foreseeable future. The aim of the plan must be the stopping of the rainfall areas losing water and becoming deserts by building up their plant and tree populations, and in the desert areas to bring pure water back into the arid lands and steadily build up their plant and tree populations and so revegetate and rebuild their desert soils.

Both sides of the plan will require a great deal of sustained and continuous energy input to make them successful in achieving the turnaround of the global environmental deterioration that is accelerating at present. It will only be achieved by the continual watching of trained human eyes and brains, and these are in extremely short supply at present in the world. It must be accepted that there is no hope of profit making from such activities for centuries to come. The scheme is working for posterity and the continuation of the species. All ecosystems will need to be balanced as well as vastly and continuously improving the symbiotic relationship with the living environment around them. This can only come about from Homo sapiens changing their ways and lifestyles by making a great deal of individual effort to carry out their part in the scheme. Greed and profit has no part in such a plan, yet with careful planning of community efforts there need not be a diminishing of the living standards for the better off, but a vast improvement for the majority of the human population.

The plan in both rainfall and non-rainfall areas will only succeed if it is done by a patchwork of small areas or micro-environments tackled by small groups in a community. The aim of each group should be the preservation of water in the soil and ensuring that it remains pure for living plants and animals to use. Once this is achieved then the group should set out to increase the number of trees in their micro-environment so that their leaf area will produce more oxygen than the plants and animals are using each day. This will be easier to achieve in rural districts but be extremely difficult in towns and cities where water in the soil and trees is already in short supply. In many such areas the necessary depopulation has already begun with people moving to the so-called "leafy" suburbs, many of which have already lost their leafiness! New centres of population need to be developed with woodlands and open spaces but no polluted ground water, where oxygen production can exceed animal demand for it. Over congested cities are a direct product of the industrial and commercial systems built up, and still continuing to be so by the present globe destroying financial system.

The small groups planning their micro-environments must work closely with one another and their surrounding groups, so as to avoid poaching each other's resources, also avoid discharging the waste products of their own schemes to the detriment of the surrounding districts. This is particularly true of water supplies, and in many areas of the globe tensions between nations, or even groups within a nation, are developing and beginning to show this in their day to day activities. The present Secretary General of the United Nations, Boutras Boutras-Ghali said "the next war in the Middle East will be fought over water, not politics" and in his previous appointment, when Egyptian Foreign Minister said, "the national security of Egypt lies in the hands of the eight other African countries in the Nile Basin." Egypt is completely dependent on the World's longest river and has been for thousands of years, the annual flooding from the mountains of

Ethiopia bringing crops and sustenance to the Egyptian people since the beginning of habitation. The world population is already using three times the amount of water it did forty years ago. The cycle of destruction is simple – cut down the trees, the springs dry up, as a tree captures the rains and allows them to seep into the soil beneath, once the trees have gone the rains run down the hillside or across the plains and strip the topsoil by erosion. This then gives rise to flooding as happens almost annually now in Bangladesh because the hillsides have been deforested in the far off Himalayas. It will only stop when the hills and mountains are replanted and the forests preserved there to retain the waters on the mountains as it falls during the monsoons.

In those locations on the globe that have adequate rainfall to keep the rivers flowing, structures must be set up to retard the flow of water down the rivers and return the retained waters to the surrounding countryside where it will keep the water table near the surface to be used by crops and trees. On most rivers the water can be retarded by weirs or small dams built at appropriate points. At these checkpoints either windpumps or wind generators can be installed and so pump the water out to the countryside through mains, then fed into the topsoil by underground irrigation pipes which can be controlled by valves. Surface irrigation, especially in warmer countries, wastes too much water by evaporation and should not be used except where specifically needed for such crops as rice. Pipe irrigation is always costly to install but is effective and provides work to install and control throughout the year to keep up the water table. The installation is much longer lasting than surface irrigation, the channels of which are easily damaged and need constant maintenance and renewal. The waters so retained along the river should be pumped back from it as far as supplies will allow and by continuing the process throughout the year, subsoil water will be built up, raising the water table and providing retaining moisture in the soil, and below in the subsoil in dry spells in the summer. The formation of arid desert locations is always speeded up because of lack of subsoil water and too low a water table for plants and trees to reach the moisture.

In each of the micro-environments set up by communities, rivers and ground water pollution must be totally eliminated in their area of control. This means no human, agricultural or industrial effluent gets into the rainwater or the groundwater and thus into rivers or streams. This simple task alone will take a great deal of human energy and will need to be a continuous process. It will involve the building and operation of sewage plants and digesters to eliminate such source of pollution, and then maintenance for effective working order will be a perpetual process, continuing until the source of pollution is eliminated. Under the present method of finance this would have to be done by local or national taxation, but under the new organisation it would be funded continuously by the SAP unit finance scheme, the grant being based on the population numbers involved in the operation and benefiting from it.

Already twenty-six countries of the world, including many in Africa and the Middle East, get less water than they need for their population numbers. In the next thirty years another forty Nations are expected to join them as their populations outstrip their rainfall and available ground waters. This will mean a third of the world's peoples are deficient of water for their everyday needs. Some, unless controlled and helped, might be driven to war to acquire their neighbour's supplies. These water deficient areas must be the first to be tackled and all available resources poured into them to build up pure water supplies by desalination, and their infrastructure developed to get water from their coasts to the arid inland areas. Once this is done then the build up of tracts of forests, woods, and ample vegetation in the inland locations will produce oxygen; moisture in the atmosphere by transpiration; and encourage precipitation of moisture back into the soil to maintain and build up the groundwater which will sustain the new environment, helped by the main water supplies from the desalination plants. All this will be a long process taking decades to achieve and continuous effort by the local populations.

Up to now water conservation in rivers has tended to be done by large dams and reservoirs, indeed these are still being built, often to the consternation of countries downstream. For instance the dams that Turkey builds on the Euphrates, give concern to Syria, who also needs the Euphrates' waters, and the dams that Syria is building give even greater concern to Iraq who is also dependent on the Euphrates' waters. In time none of the water that flows down the Euphrates will ever reach the seas of the Persian Gulf. This large scale damming is wrong because in such hot climates as the Middle East the rate of evaporation from such large water surfaces speeds up the rate of water loss, and may benefit the mountains of Iran and Afghanistan by clouds of moisture drifting away and precipitating their moisture on them, but not the immediate area of the valley of the Euphrates. Chains of weirs and small dams surrounded and shaded by tall palm trees and other types of trees, with their waters being pumped back to the surrounding top soils will be much more productive and allow water to be used along the whole length of the river. Once the valleys and local hills become covered in trees and vegetation, then more rain will occur in the valley and the precipitations will build up the soil waters. In time, in dry areas, like the Colorado in Western America, no river should discharge water into the sea except during flood periods. Hot, dry, arid cities like Khartoum and Omdurman in the central Sudan could stand in cool wooded plains, and regularly receive rainfall throughout the year, instead of a few days in midsummer as they do now, and still send enough water downstream to supply Egypt. Then humanity will know it has reversed the destruction of the globe!

As already outlined the recycling of water from small dams and weirs, going on continuously throughout the year, will maintain a high water table although some water will be still lost by that taken up and evaporated by trees and ground vegetation. To stop such soil water loss, in any part of the globe, the tendency, in the interest of higher returns by large scale mechanisation to have large fields and cultivated areas must be reversed, as this increases evaporation from the soil surfaces because of lack of shade, evaporation by drying winds and rapid runoff of rainwater, especially on sloping ground. Land must be enclosed by hedgerows containing suitable shrubs and trees for the location, in areas of ten to fifteen hectares. These enclosures using hedgerows of evergreen and deciduous shrubs to break the wind movement across soil, and their roots, will stop water movement in the soil and so reduce soil and wind erosion as at present happens in wide open fields. A large proportion of trees in the hedgerows must be allowed to develop to maturity, thus increasing the leaf area for oxygen production and the increase of moisture in the air by transpiration. To achieve this will mean less drastic use of the mechanical hedgecutter which at present eliminates large numbers of hedgerow trees when they are young, not allowing them to become big enough to be seen and left to mature. In areas where livestock is kept the shade will be of benefit in hot spells, while in rainy periods more water will be retained by the tree and hedge foliage and so help to build up the soil water in the area.

Dividing the irrigated and enclosed countryside pattern, wherever it is done will cut down wind and water erosion of the topsoil, one of the main causes of soil loss in arid areas. Cover within the hedgerows and trees forming the enclosures will provide a habitat for the natural wildlife of the area and so help to control pests that attack the crops. In Britain slugs in some areas have become a major cause of crop losses, because of the lack of hedgerows to give cover to hedgehogs and badgers to whom slugs are a major dietary item. The pellets used to control slugs are poisonous to birds and in some areas Lapwings have almost disappeared where once they were a common local bird. The micro-environment created in the ten to fifteen hectare fields will improve yields, and improve shade when livestock is in them. Crops will benefit because water evaporation by sun and wind will be reduced and more water will be available to the crop instead of the rapid drying out that can occur in wide open fields. This pattern has been proven to work in the high and low rainfall areas of the world and helps to stop the runoff of nutrients and so improve the topsoil. In the banana and rubber plantations of West Africa the early planters developing the location used Palm Kernel trees to divide the plots on the plantation into ten or fifteen hectare enclosures and so break up the violent winds that occur during the long rainy season in that region.

In hill areas across the globe suitable for growing crops and trees, the ancient art of terracing should be reintroduced where necessary to retain topsoils. Terraces will stop topsoil loss in regions of high or sudden rainfall, whereas contour ploughing as practised by the early settlers in parts of America did not and the "dust bowl" conditions of the twenties and thirties developed with the soil blowing away. Into these terraces water could be pumped from the retained weir waters in the river valleys, either into reservoirs on top of the hills or directly into the installed underground irrigation systems, thus making crop production possible where otherwise cultivated topsoils might blow or wash away. At present this is not economically attractive because of the low return on the high capital investment, but with funds being provided by the new financial organisation it will not only step up food production in these areas but also provide meaningful work for the local communities for present and future generations. Again in such areas the hills should be criss-crossed, both up and down and across with banks of trees and shrubs to provide and establish micro-environments in the terraced plots, thus helping moisture retention, their roots holding the soils and cutting down erosion, as well as the leaves providing oxygen and improving the air quality both for humans, animals and crops. If this had been done on the lower slopes of the Himalayas as the people of the areas cleared them, then their topsoils would have been retained for their own use and the rainwaters would not have rushed down the major rivers and caused the annual flooding that now occurs in Bangladesh.

Fortunately in parts of China and South East Asia the art of terracing and the communal skills involved is still practised. In an article in the *Observer Magazine* on Sunday 9th January 1994 called "The mountain sculptors of Yunnan", it was reported, quote "how the Hanai people of Tibet migrated to South West China two and a half thousand years ago and brought to a rugged pocket of Yunnan in the Ailao mountains, a new farming technique which would revolutionise agriculture throughout South East Asia, the irrigated rice terrace. By sculpting rice paddies out of the mountain sides, the Hanai were able to bring huge areas of land under cultivation." This was illustrated by brilliant photographs by Yann Lyma. "The terraces (shown on the front cover of this book) are the result of centuries of labour, and today despite the encroachment of China's new economic revolution, life in these mountains is still inexorably bound to the rice cycle. Construction takes place in February, rice is planted in May; the harvest is in September. Carving the terraces is a communal activity, and new fields are blessed and fertilised with the blood and offal of a sacrificed pig. A few miles away in the city of Yuanyang the video age has arrived, but for the time being the Hanai seem content to pursue their serene way of growing rice, worshipping the sacred buffalo, drinking rice wine, smoking tobacco through a gigantic pipe, or bong, and keeping alive their extraordinary oral tradition – they can – it is said, cite their ancestry back through 58 generations" Such a people, with grants from the new International funds could have electricity generated by wind, sun and water power, improved housing and grain storage, drainage, schools and medical facilities both Chinese and Western if they want it. And still live their ideal communal life without any further hassle of so called civilisation.

In hill areas not suitable for cropping where they do not possess enough topsoil because of their height above sea level, or the extremely high rainfall they receive such as Amazonia, then these should be reforested by trees suitable to the location. These trees will bind and improve the spare topsoils with their roots and help build up the soil and nutrients available to the trees. Much topsoil has already been lost in such locations because of man's activities. eg. in the Alps where the development of winter skiing facilities has changed the traditional relationship between mountain slopes and the inhabitants so bringing vastly increased numbers of humans into a normally inhospitable landscape, avalanche barriers now have to be erected, where previously trees would have retained the snow slips. Likewise, in Amazonia, steep slopes have been denuded of vegetation in extremely high rainfall areas and converted into grass land for beef production. However the amount of beef they produce now is hardly great enough to feed the gauchos who tend the cattle, yet alone provide beef for export to produce wealth for the growing population. Such locations should be planted with the natural trees and undercover shrubs so the moisture will be retained and the fruits and nuts produced by the replanting will produce income from sales to the outside world, in many cases providing valuable materials for medicines and natural cures across the globe. Again such plantings will stop water rushing down into the valleys to cause flooding in lower areas, as happens now in India and China.

To do all this on a world-wide scale will require a vast and rapid injection of capital into the global infrastructure from the new financial Organisation under the United Nations control. There is no possibility in the present financial structure operated by world banking of generating such wealth for capital injection. The new scheme will have to allow per head of the population sufficient units of energy to set the regeneration process off. The activation and expansion of world trade that this would generate in a short time would make the present GATT scheme of world trade look like peanuts, and the process would have to continue for an infinite period, in fact for ever and ever if the globe and the species Homo sapiens are to survive. Rural areas would have to be repopulated to set up communities to re-establish the vegetation of desert areas requiring the provision of housing, water supplies, sewage and waste disposal, renewable power supplies, health and educational facilities and local industries to maintain and supply these facilities from their own resources wherever possible. If properly planned it will reduce the overcrowding of cities and towns and enhance the living environment of the world population as well save the vital but fragile Eco-system, at present denied all this by the outdated and totally inadequate financial system.

The Eco-system plans for the globe should aim at achieving a continual improvement of the world's environment within a hundred years of the start of concerted international effort to solve the destruction of the ecology of the species. The objective should be to have pure water supplies that are ample for all plant, animal and human needs. The oxygen content of the atmosphere should have reached a level by then so the ozone layer is not only restored across the globe but increasing in thickness so as to protect the environment all the time. Then, and only then, will the damage caused by the Industrial Revolution and unbridled technology have been overcome. From then on a disciplined control of the use of the earth's resources will have to be exercised and maintained by International Law, and those communities that seek to ignore that Law will be subjected to loss of financial support and to International sanctions that stop their disobedience in its tracks. The International Police Force should be moved in to the community and their actions stopped by force if necessary. The fragile Eco-system that all species now live in, caused by the sheer numbers of the species Homo sapiens, means that destruction of the environment for individual or community gain can no longer be allowed or tolerated. This will mean a lowering of living standards for the Western Industrial World who at present use eighty percent of the earth's resources, and a vast raising of standards with the giving of economic stability to the other two thirds of the world who are living on or below starvation level. Then, and only then, will the increasing scenes of human beings scavenging for their food on waste tips be abolished from the television screens across the affluent world!

To achieve such an improvement in the Eco-system will need a complete change of social attitude and the total world-wide acceptance of truly democratic government where all views are heard and harnessed for the good of the communities, unbiased by party political views which seek to uphold one section of the community only, as present social structures encourage. The elimination and abolition of wars, except to uphold International Law and Order, must be achieved and operated in this new world order. The social motivation of the whole globe must be by the control of private wealth so it does not impose its will on fellow human beings, or other species on earth, the acceptance by all ethnic and religious groups that they have to live together in peace to maintain the fragile Eco-system they live in, and share with all other living species of fauna and flora. The overall control of this must be World Government by the United Nations made up of democratically elected member States who must accept and adhere to the control and laws of World Government in the interest of the Eco-systems. No Nation, because of its so called wealth, should regard itself as a super power and so attempt to change the course of human progress as at present happens with such powers as America, Europe, China and until recently, the Soviet Block. At all times the votes and wishes of the population masses must have supreme power to maintain and improve theirs and the globe's environment and not be constantly subjected to wealth producing interests that dominate the present economic system, irrespective of such domination's effect on the Eco-system of the world.

All this may appear impossible to achieve in the present social, ethnic, economic and religious shambolic chaos that exists at the end of the Twentieth Century. But in this post Industrial period when the devastating effect of Homo sapiens on its environment is becoming increasingly apparent to the most bigoted of politicians and economists, the promise of ample finance, stable social conditions and regular work for all the world's population to earn a steady income in global improvement, should overcome the existing tensions and encourage large and small communities to work together. At all times, once the new financial and social order is operating, people should have the right to make their views and feelings known through the ballot box by the method of peoples' or proportional representation.

Once the necessity to change the lifestyle of Homo sapiens and the use of the energy based new financial order is accepted and becomes the policy of the United Nations then the following course of action should be started:

First - Working Committees of experts in their field of activity should be established to decide, agree and publish the calorific values for all human activities, materials and essentials used in everyday life for the operations carried out. This will require experts in all human activity, food, public services, finance, construction, mining, oil and water extraction, transport including rail, sea, air and road etc., and all others that need to have fixed and agreed values for human enterprise to be used in costing. A manual for each area of activity should be published for standard use in costings, in charging and in seeking financial backing for essential and non-essential activities in the new world order. All this compilation could take ten years or longer to publish and be ready for use and must be in the languages of all Nations taking part in the scheme.

Second - All intending participants should during the setting up period, change their electoral methods and their government makeup to the people, or proportional representation method, of running their elections. When these take place they should be overseen and umpired by United Nations representatives to ensure they comply with the system laid down by them. All political views of parties polling enough votes to qualify must be represented in the government of a country, so that no single party can in future dominate their parliament. The General Assembly of the United Nations must first agree a suitable election structure based on single transferable votes to be used by all countries across the globe that wish to qualify for aid under the new financial scheme. No nation or country should qualify until they have elections supervised by the United Nations' representatives and have a Government operating that enables all parties qualifying to have a say in the running of their nation or country.

Third - Also during the setting up period the structure of the new International Bank to supervise the scheme should be established and the necessary staff recruited, trained and assembled in the member countries. During this time of establishment the population of all participating countries should be accurately determined and checked. A births and deaths registration mechanism established so qualifying population numbers for credit can be found and be ready for the issuing of funds once the bank starts to operate. From the onset of operations the issuing of currency and credit in SAP units can commence from the first day so countries can start acquiring food and other supplies to use in implementing the restructuring and environmental improvement of all member countries qualifying to take part.

Fourth - In preparation for the start of the vastly expanded world trade situation that will result from the new financial credit scheme, the United Nations and participating countries must look at and establish an International Transport Organisation. This will transfer food and other essential goods to the most needy countries so they can adequately feed their people and so give them the energy to plan and build their infrastructure of internal transport comprising of rail and road systems, and start establishing an adequate water supply. International transport be it at sea, air or rail will be central to the success of saving the Eco-system and enhancing the living standards of two thirds of the world. The International commercial mercantile section of industry has a major future in this to provide ships, railway equipment, aircraft large and small and trained personnel to carry out the huge expansion that will be necessary. Many new port facilities to handle container ships large and small will be required, adequate airports central to inland distribution systems able to handle cargo planes will be essential. All this should start to be planned and set up as soon as the United Nations decides to adopt the new finance system. Berlin in the forties, and Bosnia and now Rwanda in the nineties, have shown the inadequacies of the present methods of distribution of essential supplies in times of shortages.

Fifth - To run this whole new global scheme efficiently will require vast numbers of qualified, experienced and specially trained staff of all nationalities taking part. The United Nations already have a staffing structure across the globe for its many aid and humanitarian schemes they are at present operating. This will need to be expanded, almost in the form of a dedicated world "Army" of staff to operate the scheme impartially so that those benefiting will respect and trust the U.N. staff as being fair and helpful at all times. The expansion of this organisation and its training must be started from the passing of the United Nations first resolution to set up the scheme. It should offer a proper career structure to all who are appropriately training and eager to serve in the saving of the Eco-system and all surviving species including Homo sapiens.

Sixth - At the same time as the main administrative staffs are being set up, the United Nations should start to recruit and train an International Police or Military Force to maintain and enforce world peaceful co-operation and co-existence, especially in those areas where conflicts and suppression of peoples still exist.

Governments that are not prepared to change to the new system and not take part in the global enhancement scheme to save the Eco-system will have to be subjected to pressures by the rest of the world to make them co-operate, be it over nuclear proliferation, expansion of industry that pollute their neighbours' environs, or the suppression of living standards on secular or religious grounds. If persuasion, sanctions and peaceful means fail, then the ultimate weapon of diplomacy must be exercised; an armed force to overthrow the dissenters who are endangering the enhancement and restoration of the globe. This trained military or police force will need to be deployed across the world, based, housed and trained in those countries that are ready to have them. As they will bring greater financial benefits by having them in a country, there should be no difficulty in finding countries to do this. Perhaps the old Middle East saying of British colonial times "Behind the British Army (U.N. Force) flows a river of gold" could be transferred to the U.N. Forces because of the finance and stability in SAP units.

Seventh - Once the framework of staff to organise and run the SAP unit financial scheme is in place, then the priority of work should be to proceed to organise the new infrastructure in all participating countries to bring their social life up to the U.N. standards laid down to save and improve the Eco-system. This should be tackled area by area, and communities within those areas should work to enhance the local environs, so contributing to the global improvement towards pure water supplies and an enriched atmosphere by ensuring they all work to cut down industrial and commercial pollution at all times, planning and working to do so ad infinitum.

Eight - As the new set-up begins to work and show an improvement in social and ecological conditions, it will begin to attract non participating countries to join and help, so benefiting from being participant. It will be necessary to have a long continuous period to those activities steadily to build up the social and ecological improvements, to rectify the damage done in the past by global and industrial exploitation. In time, as the scheme's organisation improves then the stocks of vital necessities to the health and living standards, namely pure water, oxygen in the atmosphere, use of renewable energy and conservation of the earth's vital resources will be enshrined in the way of life of Homo sapiens and so for all other species that at present are suffering or endangered by the destruction of the globe's resources and environment.

Ninth - Sustained pressure will be necessary at this stage of development to be exerted on all countries that refuse to join the scheme until they agree to do so and include their area of the globe and their activities in the major act of saving the ecology of the earth and its fragile Eco-system for all. There are many ways of doing this; by excluding their products from the general freeing of world trade that the new finance system will bring, sanctions and severe economic pressure on the obstructive government may also be necessary and possible force where humanitarian activities are delayed or looted. In cases like Bosnia and Somalia where local "warlords" attempt to subject their populations to hardship and shortages compared with the participating countries of the world, the proposed Police or armed forces of the U.N. may have to intervene and install an interim Government to open up the way for the country to join the global scheme.

Tenth - To ensure the continual enhancement of the Eco-system the eventual and continual aim of the United Nations should be to persuade Nations, communities, families and individuals to cut back on the rate of reproduction in the human species, so cutting the demand on the earth's resources. This will raise many objections from certain religious sections of society whose teachings at the moment oppose contraception and the limitation of family sizes in spite of the financial difficulties it causes. The availability of contraception and teaching its proper use must be continuous and free to all as an environmental protection measure. Religious scruples against it must be ridiculed and it made obvious how unbridled reproduction will eventually lead to the destruction of the ecology that Homo sapiens needs to exist. Contraception must be accepted and understood by the young at the time they become adolescent, so that all who wish to exercise their body's function and right to sexual activity can do so by taking precautions to avoid sexually transmitted diseases and unwanted reproduction that endangers the earth. The increased financial burdens that it gives them as individuals and their community must be pointed out, such as extra feeding, education and waste disposal that follows reproduction. It is not the intention to advocate promiscuity in society but the recognition of the species Homo sapiens as a member of the animal Kingdom, using the fragile earth's Eco-system, and having the natural inbuilt aspirations to be able to partake of sexual activity, but not, in so doing, in the earth's interest, always to reproduce.

Only when all this balanced control of the world's Eco-system is operating and being properly maintained unto posterity, will the right environmental balance be apparent to all who live in it. The greedy demands for profit and exploitation of the globe's resources, without replacement, as the present financial system allows, will never achieve this if it is continued, so change is essential and the sooner the better.

- 10 -

Training And Education
To Perpetuate The New Stability

Once the United Nations General Assembly has accepted the need and urgency of introducing the new financial system to save and enhance the global environment, then the greatest task to be tackled is the training of those who are to set up and operate the scheme. First, as always, those who are to do the training will have to be trained, and become dedicated to carry out this first vital phase of the scheme. They will need to be committed to the whole concept because there will be a great deal of opposition to the change, especially from those vested interests such as politicians and possibly bankers and financiers who see their present grip on the world infrastructure and social structure being eroded and disposed of. The training of the trainers will take time and will need very careful planning, because it will be important to train enough personnel to take the explanation of training to all corners of the globe. Alongside this initial training, thought must be given to the necessity to educate and train future generations through schools, colleges and Universities on how the environmental necessity for change arose, and how it must be maintained ad infinitum. There is a need to reiterate this cause for change during the setting up period and to the future rising generations.

The U.N. administration must decide how the policy of training, and the details to be included in it, will operate. The object of the policy must be to restore and permanently enhance the Eco-system of the globe, and to offer to all human beings basic human rights including an adequate diet throughout the year, pure water to drink and clean air to breathe; adequate and good housing serviced by efficient drainage and waste disposal; cheap and sufficient power supplies; a transport system that brings supplies into the community and takes their saleable products out; a properly resourced medical service together with a basic and advanced education service. Initially experienced staff in all these fields of activity will need to be recruited and appointed on long

105

term contracts so they can dedicate their future lives to the policy, these appointees will need training in the details of the whole scheme. Specialist sections of the Organisation should especially address the detail of the financial operation, all aspects of environmental enhancement, and all aspects of the new social basic provisions listed above. All involved in this training should see and accept the aim of reversing the destruction of the globe's resources with the rapid improvement of the environment around the world.

Once the detail of the education and training policy has been broadly worked out and publicised, then the next stage is to enlist and engage the help in running courses in all participating countries. This will involve courses at Universities, Colleges of Technology and equivalent Education Establishments, so that suitable candidates can be selected, educated and trained, and from whom eventually the United Nations' representatives doing the appointment of staff will be able to recruit according to the student's achievements in the courses. These recruits may not be wanted in their own countries but could be posted elsewhere in the world where the demand for their training was needed. By having courses running across the world this will provide a reservoir of trained and interested personnel who may have a range of languages that enables them to work elsewhere in the world where those languages are spoken. Staff from other countries working for the United Nations schemes tend to be more impartial and unbiased than if working in their own country of origin, though obviously some staff must be indigenous to that country to ensure a thorough understanding of problems.

The education and training courses must be for all levels of ability, not just the management recruitment. By far the largest recruitment must be at technical level to make the scheme work efficiently, as they will be needed actually to carry out the whole programme on the ground in participating countries. The training of operators in the field will mainly be for the local work force as this will be where the greatest provision of employment will be in the scheme. The actual Advisory or Consultant staffs' jobs will include the assessment of the environmental damage at the start of the scheme and the suggested steps to reverse the damage done; so helping to lay down the plans needed to commence the improvement of the environment. In many countries across the world these consultancy skills already exist though they may need to attend a course on the exact aims of the new enhancement programme and the financial scheme to back it. These first Advisors or Consultants must have accepted the need to change Global improvement and be prepared to dedicate a lot of time in doing it; otherwise the initial setting up may be flawed and sabotaged by outsiders or the present vested interests.

As the National, Regional and local branches of the new Banking structure is recruited and put into position across the areas, they will have to be trained to assume the responsibility for training the local population in the use of the new energy costing methods. This will be part of the necessary programmes to familiarise the areas in the financial benefits under the new scheme, and how they are to submit applications for new grants to improve their local infrastructure and to commence the improvement of the local environs to meet the new standards. The substitution of the new SAP unit into existing costing procedures using the tables of calorific values produced by the various working committees should not be too difficult to teach to those who have to operate it in their everyday business life. The procedure of costing and price fixing will be the same as they use at present, but instead of cost fixing in local currency they will be using the calorific values that will be stable in value, not fluctuating like the present local monetary unit. The advantages of this must be obvious to anyone experienced in budgeting, costing and price fixing operations.

Mass education of the human population must start right from the acceptance of the scheme to save the Eco-system and the earth's environment, by the United Nations Organisation. The impossibility of continuing to exploit the earth by the present mode of living must be explained to emphasise that Homo sapiens cannot go on living like this, to quote Mikhail Gorbachov. The method of mass education must be through the popular media including the press, radio and television; each of these must initially include a fair percentage of their programmes telling the message that all ways of living have got to change, this can be reduced a little once   changes have begun. Other established Services must also join in the education process including national Education Services, Government and local Bodies especially those that are constantly sending information to their members, all must point out the vital importance of reversing the treatment of global resources. Important key areas of global damage must be included and how to be constantly recycling all possible materials, of stopping even the most simple acts of pollution such as smoke production from the simplest cigarettes used by the individual to the mass burning of forests as a means of land clearance; they all use oxygen. The more complex acts of pollution must also be emphasised, especially if there are radiation dangers or chemical pollution of groundwater from such places as tips and drain outlets. Cutting the use of oxygen out of the atmosphere and water out of the ground also must figure in the education campaign as well as the rebuilding of the tree and shrub populations; soil conservation and the reclaiming of arid areas by building up the soil waters across the world. The vast arid areas across large sections of all continents must be vegetated and eliminated from the world's media screens, then the enhancement of the earth's resources will have begun, because often it is Homo sapiens who has eliminated those areas' original vegetation.

Continual explanation must be given for the necessity to switch rapidly from fossil fuels, all of which require the consumption of oxygen to release their stored energies, to renewable fuels, or energy giving sources as has already been outlined. Air movement, water movement and the sun's heat must be central to this explanation, especially emphasising the sun's part in the activation of the environment on the earth. Most people do not seem to realise this at the end of the twentieth century, so removed have many become from their natural environment – yet every domestic or wild cat knows when to sit in the sun to recharge it's health batteries! The dangers of continuing to be dependent on the modern internal combustion engine for so much power used in the world today must be emphasised in that it has become a vast consumer of oxygen in its present form and a vast polluter of the atmosphere by producing an excess of the dangerous carbon dioxide and monoxides. It is not beyond the wit of man (or woman) to produce a non-oxygen consuming source of mobile power to serve man's purposes – there is an excess of high energy plutonium in the world, which does not use oxygen to produce its power and which can be rendered comparatively safe from its radiation dangers; here is a vast scope for man's ingenuity and inventiveness. The urgent necessity to stop using trees for domestic fuel for cooking, especially charcoal, must be emphasised, except where the tree crops have been specially grown for use as fuel and are being constantly replaced. All timber waste products should either be converted into building products ie. chipboard, or shredded to put back on the soil as organic dressing to improve and enhance free drainage of soils.

The average member of the public would soon come to accept the need for action and investment to save the fragile but vital Eco-system that all species live in, especially if the dangers of the present human lifestyle, both in the third world and the energy consuming Western one, are constantly pointed out. All Education means available must be used to do this before the new financial and environmental organisation is introduced and implemented, otherwise vested and political interests will do all in their power to stop the changes taking place. There is a vast range of those who will oppose moving away from their present personally lucrative modus operandi; the existing motor manufacturers; the oil, gas and coal supply organisations; those private interests that at present control water supplies; the drug and the armament trade on all of which the present economic system depends, will not want to see vital changes made. The general public must be convinced that change to a financial system aimed at stopping and restoring the earth's environment can be done and in doing so provide them with work, that a stable lifestyle which supplies their basic needs is possible and achievable if all nations work towards such a goal.

Throughout a child's period of schooling and then right through adult life there must be a reiteration of the importance of environmental enhancement and maintenance, so that the problem is in the forefront of their thinking. People need to be constantly reminded of how the destruction of the Eco-system rapidly developed during the short period of the Industrial Age when the consequences of ignoring the needs of the environment and other species were imposed on the earth's resources to meet the requirements of a fast growing human population. Once environmental improvement starts then the emphasis must be on how to avoid returning to that disastrous situation. Constant repetition of how individuals can contribute by their own personal actions that cut out waste, pollution, contamination and excessive demands for scarce commodities must be emphasised by the media and the Education Services; the selfishness of excessive eating, becoming obese and not keeping fit, by avoiding self inflicted health risks by not smoking, excessive drinking of alcohol and especially by not taking or using drugs! There is an essential requirement for the world population to get back to basics to quote a much misused phrase of the last decade of the twentieth century, but in the true sense of the phrase it means living in harmony with one's environment, not overpopulating it and so creating excessive demands on finite resources.

To all age groups the education process must constantly emphasise the vital need to control and reduce the human population, so that the earth's resources will continue to be adequate to meet their basic needs. The teaching of contraception among the reproductive age group across the world is a first priority, and free contraception must be available to this age group. Medical science must stop trying to play God in wasting resources of time, skills and money on making the infertile fertile, and those past childbearing age to be able to bear yet another child to make demands on the earth's resources. There are plenty who are already here who need those resources. The need to limit family size must be tied in with both the personal financial aspect and the need to cut excessive demands on environmental availability in any education programme. From now on Global protection is much more important than individual freedom to reproduce itself.

The delicate balance between the fragile Eco-system and the size of the human population is now at the stage where any dramatic increase in that population can only accelerate the use of essential resources, leading to increasing numbers of confrontations as is happening in the human population already; Bosnia, Somalia, Angola and now Southern Mexico and Rwanda are strong manifestations of this frightening trend. Future generations must be taught to recognise the danger of this situation to the future of the species, a cut back in the excessive use of energy, be it machines of war, the rapid travelling of great distances, the overuse of heating and lighting in some city areas are all dangers that must be comprehended and understood by mankind. The new financial organisation is directed at slowing down the pace of living and moving more at the pace of the natural cycle of life, so human energy, not the excessive demands of machines govern the speed at which work and improvement can be carried out. Stress due to the excessive demands of working and living is the twentieth century growth disease, no Nation demonstrates this more than America, where modern management teaching resulting from the present economic system epitomises the stupidity of mankind in his rush to destroy the world's resources. What is needed is a return to a living natural environment with a social order that moves in harmony with it, not governed by excessive greed for unnecessary wealth based on global destruction. Future generations should aim for a simpler, easier lifestyle not motivated by the need to generate artificial wealth from the earth's resources that cannot be renewed, but moving at the natural pace of nature improving and enhancing the life giving cycles of pre-industrial days. Think of the Hanai people of Southern China who have survived two and a half thousand years probably without a single foreign loan!

As already mentioned, future national examinations in all Educational Establishments should include papers on environmental enhancement and restoration to a level where it will sustain the Eco-system. The knowledge that needs to be tested right across the globe, should include the control of the energy use by budgeting and costing its use, the methods of recycling and avoiding pollution of air, water and land resources, so that future generations know the dangers of their lifestyle to the earth and to succeeding generations. Advancement to higher qualifications should be stopped if the environmental papers are not passed. No one should be exempt from acquiring this vital knowledge.

Part of the environmental education being instituted by the United Nations should be to encourage, world-wide, a scheme whereby all school leavers should be encouraged to serve a period in the service of the U.N. Global Enhancement Scheme, preferably in a country other than their own and in disciplines other than the one they intend to follow as a career. What started as the "Grand Tour" of the young wealthy centuries ago, and has now become the "Year between" school and University, could become part of their training and understanding of the environment, so broadening their outlook on its problems. It should be a form of paid International Service for widening their knowledge of practical environmental work, and giving them an opportunity to travel and understand other nations' ways of life in environs other than their own.

The eventual aim of such a programme should be to give to all the world's young, who have their lives in front of them, a wide knowledge of the globe's environment, of how to maintain it and a chance so they appreciate the importance of their individual action on this environment. All who are prepared to work together and give their abilities to the community and other fellow human beings, should be rewarded by the new financial system while they continue to work for the good of all. All disabled who are unable to work should be entitled to the same basic rights and not be penalised by their disabilities, it should no longer be necessary for those so unfortunate to have to beg, as such vast numbers have to at present. The only ones excluded from the scheme are those connected with, and convicted of crimes against society, fraud and armed robbery or insurrection, because society must be protected from such peoples.

One thing that has got to change in the attitude to education right across the world is the size of the reward to those responsible for the education of present and future generations. They should be recognised and rewarded as being one of the most important groups in society, an elite group of dedicated people, who in future, once the scheme is working will be responsible for the future of the species. The rewards offered, and their conditions of service should be great enough to attract the best brains available nationally. To maintain standards of teaching and organisation they should, of course be subject to strict disciplines and inspections continually to maintain and improve their work and presentation, provided with the best teaching aids available and not subjected to outside pressures from political parties who may want to play down environmental issues in the curriculum.

The success or failure of the new financial scheme organised by the United Nations depends on the training and education of all involved in setting it up and then operating it fairly in all Nations and countries who wish to participate. The proper organisation and the sustained high standards of recruitment of the best brains available across the world is imperative for this is a way of life that has to run and run, as long as human society manages to exist. This means job security and long term contracts are essential for making the scheme work efficiently. The present stupid system in America and Britain of so called "Market Forces" and short term contracts has no place in long term environmental projects the world needs today. The breakdown of the existing financial system has been accelerated in the last twenty years of the twentieth century by the ridiculous and inappropriate use of short terms of employment. Employees do not see themselves having a real place in the scheme of things and so do not give of their best to an organisation or business. This is not the way to preserve the earth's resources or save the species. Properly educated and trained employees and management who want to establish and maintain efficiency of their efforts are the only way forward in the twenty first century., to reverse the destruction of the fragile Eco-system so that Homo sapiens and all other species have the environment to exist in.

The Way To Achievement

The Statutes under which the United Nations Charter operates say that they will not interfere in the internal running of any member Nation. That was relevant fifty years ago before the pressures of the world population explosion started to decimate global resources. There is an urgent need now to alter the Statutes if the proposal for the new Financial Unit and Organisation is introduced, so that only true democracies can join the membership of the scheme. From now on Mixed Party Government must become the norm, elected by the peoples, or proportional representation. This will ensure that all views are represented and one party dominance should become a thing of the past. All voters, whatever their colour, creed and political views should feel they have a say in the Government of their country or areas. To achieve this will mean a change in the Statutes under which the United Nations' Organisation was set up at the end of the Second World War.

If the people of the world are to work together as a vast community, all receiving equal basic rights, enhancing and saving their fragile Eco-system then there is no longer a place for political views, bigoted, dictatorial or otherwise, and political parties wishing to impose their one-sided views on their fellow men. They must become as outdated as the Dinosaurs and the use of fossil fuels. The necessary disciplined fight to save and enhance the environment and the human species cannot afford to tolerate the corruption and deception that are the trademarks through the ages of politics and political parties. From the ancient Greeks, through the stabbing of Caesar at the Forum, right up to modern Britain and America and elsewhere, where there are political views there is deception so in order to obtain control of finance, and greed and corruption follow. As Lord Acton (1834-1902) said in his Historical Essays and studies Appendix: "Power tends to corrupt, and absolute power corrupts absolutely. Great men are almost always bad men."

Such drastic but necessary changes will be violently opposed by the existing politicians and their parties, in and out of power. The financial rewards of power are tremendous, right across the world, otherwise people would not seek to shoulder the huge responsibilities of high office. In recent times there have been many examples of how the powerful are more than amply rewarded, from Marcos of the Philippines to Gorbachov of Russia and corrupt European politicians in Italy or elsewhere, or the military Juntas of Burma and Nigeria. One good thing that comes out of pressures and publicity exerted by the modern media is that comments are flashed across the airwaves and screens of the globe, these are beginning to expose underhand or corruptive activities that half a century ago would not have been mentioned. In recent times in Britain a succession of Ministers has resigned because of exposure, mainly from one party, when politicians tried to hide they were not exactly "lily white" in their private lives. Already in Britain measures are being introduced to try to give central control to Law Enforcement by the use of a Criminal Prosecution Service controlled by the Home Office and now an attempt to make the Chairmen of Police Authorities appointees of the Government. Such steps are dangerous political manoeuvres to stop local opinion controlling local events in a community. Control of the media is also being threatened if they fail to regulate their own behaviour properly.

The controlling interests of Industry and Commerce will also strongly object to the International controls that restrict their attacks on the environment whether intentional or unintentional, especially in such fields of pollution and waste disposal because it adds to their costs. One great example of this at the moment is the cleaning up of the beaches in the Southwest, where raw sewage is continually discharged into the sea, irrespective of the health hazards it is causing on the beaches. The private water company whose responsibility it is to clean up those beaches, while paying high salaries to its Directors and big dividends to its shareholders, pleads it has to charge more for its services to consumers, rather than raise more capital sums needed to carry out the work. This type of situation cannot go on and the new financial system, besides investing the capital needed, would also lower the salaries of directors and the dividends to an average reasonable figure. The Environment and Homo sapiens cannot afford such monopolies in the future. There is a need for the scaling down of such private monopolies who cannot control essential nutrients such as water, so that they are always environmentally friendly and deliver their products into homes of consumers at an affordable price. If not, then their profits should be retained and returned to the good of the communities they serve, by a direct crippling taxation on the individuals and companies concerned.

Political parties have always relied for existence, upon subscriptions from the larger firms of Industry and Commerce world-wide. These payments made to further their own ends and business interests, often result in their being included in the Honours lists. It has recently come to light that much of the overseas aid given by the British Government in the last decade has had strings attached to it so that firms that received the contract were ones that had a large subscription giving history to the ruling party of the time. Such actions must by International Law be made illegal and confiscated. Under the new system there is a need for a level playingfield in all activities and allocation of such contracts or in the selection of candidates for local or national elections. All candidates should receive equal support and a fixed allowance from central funds both to stand as candidates and to run their campaigns. The vast sums that are spent in America and Britain, and elsewhere are both immoral and insupportable at this time when the need to invest in environmental improvement is so essential.

To control such misuse of funds after every election all campaign candidates must publish properly audited income and expense sheets. If irregularities occur and are discovered by the returning officer or the United Nations umpires then the election shall be declared null and void. Once elected, candidates should be forbidden to follow party lines and all votes and decisions on issues be without any party whips, as happens at present when party lines are always followed. Anyone attempting to change another person's intention on voting should be sacked and not

116

allowed ever to stand again. In this way the results of votes in mixed party councils or governments will be on the merits of the issue under consideration, not the party line on such issues. This is what democracy is about, government by the people for the people – not a minority section of the people. It will at least avoid the terrible mistakes being made across a globe by minorities at the moment.

The commercial International Banking community is not likely to oppose the introduction of a fixed value monetary unit because it will simplify their operations once the changeover has taken place. It will do away with the continual fluctuations that at present bedevil the money markets and make International trade easier. If they do oppose it then it is likely to stem from a failure of communications in not making them realise the benefits to themselves and to the prosperity of the whole world by the use of the scheme. By basing the monetary units available on any one day according to the world population on that day, and fairly allocated across all participating nations, this must lead to a vast increase in the number of fixed value units in circulation, and in the amount of trade in the world that commercial banks have to deal with. It will reverse the present trend of cutting down bank staffs across the globe, because extra staff will be needed to cope with the trade. The banks will have a vital part in passing International information on trading to their individual customers, and in advising them on their costing and pricing techniques with the new SAP units based on energy needs. Banking opposition to the scheme will probably only come from those engaged in "laundering" illegally obtained funds, the source of which might not be accountable for, because of their illegality.

Before countries enter the scheme the benefits of entry must be explained to the whole population by unbiased spokespersons, not from political parties, the commercial or banking world or from any religious sects. Then a referendum must be held to give every individual of 18 years or over the chance to vote on the issue. The pros and cons must be explained clearly and umpires from the United Nations have the right to interfere if biased arguments are put in front of the electorate. It must clearly be shown how the new Monies available to the area could be used, the improvements to the local environs that could result, the cutdown on taxes that they have to pay at present, because the new scheme gives them such money as an entitlement according to the local population numbers. The increase in jobs that will result will not be confined to offices and factories but those actually working on environmental improvements, be it construction work, installation of services such as water and drainage, and the maintenance of all these ad infinitum once it is all working.

Once the new financial scheme has been operating in an area then the benefits will steadily become apparent to all sections of the communities. These voters will have the power by truly democratic machinery to eliminate from positions of authority those whose actions try to restrict the basic humanitarian rights of every individual. In Britain in the last decade and a half there have been those in authority who ignored the wishes of the majority of the voting population. Government was elected by 42% of the votes cast while 58% voted against their proposals, so there has been a series of debacles, the poll tax was introduced, costing vast sums of taxpayers money then withdrawn, and those who imposed the tax were not made to pay for their mistakes; the majority of voters had to pay for something they did not support. The same imposition is being carried out on one of the essentials of life; warmth; by the imposing of value added tax on heating fuels. Under the new scheme of finance there must be unbiased Ombudsmen appointed by the United Nations and working through the International Bank who will be available to hear appeals against injustice and financial losses imposed by individuals. Parliamentarians should be made to pay for their expensive mistakes in future.

The Ombudsmen should investigate complaints and then bring injustices to the attention of the Government and to the United Nations Central Supervisory Organisation, thus political, Industrial or Commercial opposition to the granting of humanitarian rights can be met head on, and settled in the International Courts as a right to every voter. Such cases as the charges for water supplies or the cleaning up of beaches from sewage pollution would be dealt with in the future. If the Ombudsmen find the case is proven and justified then the courts can impose fines or even confiscation of trading rights on the individual or firm involved. In extreme cases the fines should be great enough to put the individuals or firms involved out of business.

As the new financial scheme progresses and social and environmental improvements begin to show in the state of the Eco-system the opposition to the changes should steadily die down. The United Nations and the participating countries should be vigilant, even at this stage, against the old destructive and corrupt methods creeping back into the global scene. At any time the central banking organisation must have the right to audit specific schemes or the whole improvement plans for the area or country. Participants should understand on joining that this can occur at any time without prior notice through the Regional or Area Branches of the International Bank. These Branches should be constantly monitoring the progress of improvement and where countries are failing to meet their predicted and agreed targets of social and environmental improvement, then there will be a need to decide if extra aid is needed and given as necessary. Climatic or geological problems could well cause a project to fall behind schedule especially where materials or equipment are not readily available.

Time is not on the side of those wishing to continue the present chaotic system of finance based on environmental destruction. The lack of work for large sections of the community; the shortage of money in people's pockets as a result of higher taxation being continually imposed to raise cash to meet basic expenditure needs; increasing availability of drugs to ease people's mental and physical anguish; and the turn to armed crime resulting in the rising death rate. These are all manifestations of the chaos of the present finance system. No amount of political or religious exhortations will change the trend, the sheer weight of population increases are accelerating the trend. Only a complete change of the social and financial structure can reverse the trend and meet the needs of the oppressed and distressed masses of the world population. In Northern Ireland, Bosnia, Somalia, South Africa, Rwanda and elsewhere the vocal sections of communities are taking arms to change the system they live under, and their protests are being seen constantly on the world screens and heard on the airwaves.

Any opposition by the existing vested and corrupt interests must be swept aside and the basic human rights of all individuals, born to the species Homo sapiens, should be given to them by a fair economic system, based on the use of energy. At the same time all must be taught to recognise their place in the Eco-system of the globe, the leaf areas of the globe that produced the vital 21% of oxygen in the atmosphere must be restored and maintained by the continual planting of trees and shrubs in all areas that now are barren and denuded of vegetation. Pure, unpolluted water must be available on tap to all households and families, not four hours walk away as it is to some at present. It is reported that a woman in an African village was visited by a health advisor who told her that her children should wash their hands after going to the toilet; her reply was "I will kill anyone who uses water to wash their hands when I spend four hours a day walking to fetch it." All these improvements can be achieved, and more, if the world communities wish it to be, the so called rich must share and help the obviously poor and deprived, or face armed insurrection and terrorism as is happening everywhere already from America to China.

A very active and strong United Nations Organisation, building on the experiences it has gained in the past forty five years is the only way to unite the communities of the world to save the environment in a condition fit for Homo sapiens to continue living. The present imbalance of the distribution of resources cannot go on, especially in the face of the growing arms trade and the world-wide availability of lethal arms to people who wish to highjack world trade, which can only lead to an increase in the destruction of global resources. A change in the financial system giving agreed basic human rights to all is the only way forward. There is just time to achieve this and unite all communities of the world, but only just. Too much delay now, and it will be too late to place the new scheme into action across the globe. The damage will be too great to repair.

This old "hodge" saw colonial rule failing in the Sudan and Eritrea nearly fifty years ago, through lack of finance to give support in famine and the basic essentials of life. The situation there and elsewhere has become far worse due to population increase, shortage of food and water, wars, and lack of currency to put the situation right. What exists now is far worse than then. He has written down his reasoned solution while there is still enough oxygen in the atmosphere to make it possible! – The human situation in the last decade of the twentieth century reminds one of the story of the man sitting on a high bough of a tree, sawing it off between himself and the tree's trunk – he did not live to tell what he did wrong! If there is a future for Homo sapiens they have to change their ways "We cannot go on living like this."

Bibliography

Page

46 Calorific Values. Any supermarket book giving calorific values.

48 Election Table. The Electoral Reform Society, 6 Chancel Street, Blackfriars, London, SE1 0UU.

54 World Statistics World Watch Institute Report "*Vital Signs in 1993*" found in any good Reference Library.

95 Observer Magazine Article "The mountain sculptors of Yunnan" published on Sunday 9th January 1994.